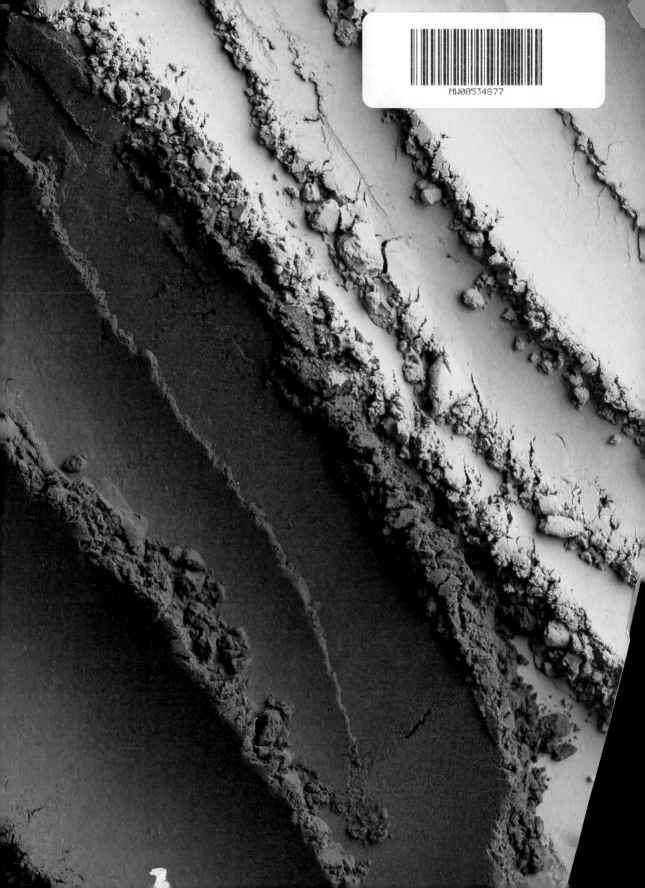

CHOCOLATE LOVER

A BAKING BOOK

MICHELE SONG

CHRONICLE BOOKS
SAN FRANCISCO

Library of Congress Cataloging-in-Publication Data available.

ISBN 978-1-7972-1591-4

Manufactured in China.

FSC
www.fsc.org
MIX
Paper | Supporting
responsible forestry
FSC™ C136333

Design by Lizzie Vaughan.
Typesetting by Wynne Au-Yeung.
Typeset in Radikal and TSTAR Mono Round.

10 9 8 7 6 5 4 3 2 1

Chronicle books and gifts are available at special quantity discounts
to corporations, professional associations, literacy programs, and other
organizations. For details and discount information, please contact our
premiums department at corporatesales@chroniclebooks.com or at
800-759-0190.

Chronicle Books LLC
Second Street
Francisco, California 94107
chroniclebooks.com

To my mom, for sparking my love for food and nurturing my passions, and to my husband, for always supporting my wildest dreams without hesitation.

CONTENTS

MY LOVE LETTER TO CHOCOLATE

Chocolate is undoubtedly one of life's simple pleasures. A universal symbol of happiness, it has the power to make ordinary moments extraordinary. It has captured the hearts of people across the globe with its rich, indulgent taste and ability to make everything just a little sweeter. Few foods, if any, are as ubiquitous and beloved by people all over the world.

In fact, I like to think of chocolate as sprinkled throughout all our lives, often playing a central role in some of our most cherished moments. Perhaps it was Grandma's fudgy chocolate cake you requested for every birthday or milestone celebration. Maybe it was the heart-shaped box of chocolates you received from your first crush on Valentine's Day. The coveted Halloween candy you'd eagerly count and strategically trade after a night of trick-or-treating. The cream-filled chocolate eggs you'd hunt on Easter or the chocolate gold gelt you'd get during Hanukkah.

Chocolate is my love language. A guilty pleasure for some, a daily ritual for me. Nothing compares to the sweet aroma of chocolate filling your kitchen and warming your soul. With just one bite of your favorite chocolate treat, any day can be made brighter, and all worries are washed away. A moment of solace and bliss. That is the magic of chocolate—it delivers happiness and joy in its purest form (which must explain the chocolate I've got stashed in my nightstand).

My love affair with chocolate began at a young age. Ever since I can remember, chocolate has been a part of my life, inextricably woven into the memories of my childhood. It not only reminds me of moments that I will forever cherish but also of the people I love.

Every holiday, my mom would set out cards for me and my brother on the kitchen table. They were always accompanied with pieces of chocolate—assorted See's Candies for Christmas, chocolate kisses for Valentine's Day, and Cadbury Creme Eggs and chocolate bunnies for Easter. It was her way of saying *I love you*. I also remember the box of chocolate ice cream bonbons my grandma and grandpa would buy every time I came to visit. I looked forward to my bonbons and always felt so special because they were just for me. Needless to say, chocolate is very near and dear to my heart.

I'd even venture to say that my journey into baking can be derived from my love of chocolate and one singular dish. Unlike most kids, I traded in my Saturday morning cartoons for PBS cooking shows. I grew up watching Jacques Pepin, Julia Child, and Jacques Torres and never missed a single episode.

When I was ten years old, my favorite show was *Dessert Circus with Jacques Torres*. I was fascinated by his creativity. For my birthday, my aunt gifted me a copy of his cookbook, which was a compilation of all the recipes from his TV show. I distinctly remember the first recipe I tried was for his edible chocolate bowls to hold sorbet or ice cream. They were made by dipping balloons into melted chocolate and then popping them once the chocolate had set. From that moment on, I was hooked. I spent every weekend baking and experimenting in the kitchen and fantasized about going to pastry school in Paris one day.

Besides those edible chocolate bowls, my entry into the world of baking had very humble beginnings. The first things I baked were of the boxed or premade variety. Ghirardelli's boxed brownies, Nestlé's cookies from the recipe on the chocolate chip bag, and boxed yellow cake with canned chocolate frosting. As I gained more confidence in the kitchen, I moved on to recipes from my mom's Betty Crocker cookbook.

Suffice to say that what started as a mild curiosity quickly grew into an obsession that has continued to bloom over the years. I discovered that baking fuels my incessant desire to create something and express myself, to color outside the lines and never stop learning or experimenting. Even in those early days, baking became my form of therapy, and it still is today.

Fast-forward twenty years, and I finally decided to fulfill my dream of going to pastry school after feeling unsatisfied with my career in finance. I quit my corporate job and moved to San Francisco. (Not quite the Paris dreams I originally had, but good enough.) After pastry school, I interned at Manresa Bread under the tutelage of Chef Avery Ruzicka. I worked on the pastry team, learning about laminated pastries, cookies, cakes, and how to use time and temperature as an ingredient. It was an invaluable experience I'll never forget. Soon after completing my internship, I decided to start my baking blog, *Studio Baked*, as a way to share my knowledge and personal recipes. Now here I am writing this book and feeling grateful to be living my dream. I owe it all to those chocolate bowls.

And so this cookbook is my love letter to chocolate dedicated to all my fellow chocolate lovers—a tribute to and celebration of chocolate in all its forms, including white chocolate, caramelized white chocolate, milk chocolate, semisweet chocolate, and dark chocolate. Inside this book, you will find sixty recipes for cakes, cookies, brownies, sweet breads, pastries, and more. Or, shall I say, sixty ways to say I love you.

Chocolate is so versatile, with its nuanced flavors, and it can be used in myriad ways. As such, I've included a primer on chocolate detailing the differences between cocoa powders and chocolate varieties. You will also find a guide to ganache and its endless flavor variations and applications such as frosting, filling, and truffles. In addition, I've sprinkled in a few tips and tricks for melting, measuring, and working with chocolate.

Whether you're looking for unfussy treats you can make in a pinch, big weekend baking projects, or elegant desserts to celebrate special occasions, you'll find recipes to satisfy all your chocolate cravings, organized by type. I've developed a variety of recipes ranging from revamped timeless classics and nostalgic childhood treats to elevated showstoppers and bucket-list bakes. The recipes range from minimal effort, like the Brown Butter–Chocolate Crispy Treats, to the more involved, like the Chocolate Crémeux Éclairs. Some of these recipes are intense, decadent chocolate bombs, while others show a bit more restraint with just hints and whispers of chocolate.

Ultimately, my goal is to share my undying love for chocolate with everyone. In creating this collection, I wanted to ensure that the recipes were accessible to all bakers, regardless of your level of experience. That's why you'll find an array of recipes ranging from simple and quick treats to more complex and challenging creations. Each recipe has been carefully crafted to provide clear instructions, helping you achieve the best results and gain confidence in your baking abilities. My hope is that this cookbook becomes your new go-to chocolate resource that you and your family come back to time and again while making your own sweet memories with chocolate.

So, fellow chocolate lover, let us embark on this delightful adventure together. Grab your apron, preheat your oven, and let's get baking!

CHOCOLATE AND COCOA VARIETIES

Before we embark on this chocolate adventure together, let's discover the incredible diversity and unique magic behind the various types of chocolate. Each variety boasts its own allure, offering distinct flavor profiles, textures, and nuanced characteristics. From the bold depth of dark chocolate to the creamy sweetness of white chocolate and everything in between, this beloved ingredient offers endless possibilities for indulgence. Understanding the complexities each type of chocolate brings to baking will empower you to choose the right chocolate for your desserts.

White Chocolate

Containing cocoa butter, sugar, and milk solids, white chocolate lacks cocoa solids, giving it a pale ivory color and a mild, creamy flavor. Its high sugar content and delicate notes of cocoa butter make it ideal for sweeter, milder desserts.

Caramelized White Chocolate

This is white chocolate that has been gently heated to caramelize its sugars, resulting in a butterscotch flavor with a distinctive caramel hue. Its unique taste adds depth and complexity to a wide range of desserts. You can find a recipe on page 18.

Milk Chocolate

Combining cocoa solids, cocoa butter, sugar, and milk solids, milk chocolate boasts a creamy, mild chocolate flavor with a sweeter taste.

Semisweet Chocolate

Semisweet chocolate contains cocoa solids, cocoa butter, and sugar, with a slightly lower sugar content than milk chocolate. This well-balanced chocolate offers a pleasant mix of sweetness and cocoa flavor, making it a staple in many dessert recipes.

Dark Chocolate

Containing a higher percentage of cocoa solids and cocoa butter with less sugar, dark chocolate offers a more intense, robust chocolate flavor. Its varying cocoa percentages allow for customization in terms of bitterness and depth, suiting a wide array of dessert preferences. More often than not, dark chocolate is my go-to for chocolate desserts.

Bittersweet Chocolate

Bittersweet chocolate is a type of dark chocolate with an even higher percentage of cocoa solids, resulting in a more pronounced, bolder chocolate flavor. Ideal for those who enjoy a slightly bitter edge, bittersweet chocolate adds intensity and sophistication to desserts.

Unsweetened Chocolate

Composed solely of cocoa solids and cocoa butter, unsweetened chocolate is devoid of sugar, providing an intense, pure cocoa flavor. This chocolate type is primarily used in recipes where sugar is added separately, allowing for precise control over sweetness levels.

COCOA POWDER VARIETIES

Cocoa powder, derived from cacao beans, is a key ingredient that brings depth, color, aroma, and that distinct fudgy chocolate flavor to your baked goods. With its high percentage of cocoa solids and concentrated chocolate flavor, this seemingly humble ingredient is capable of transforming and enhancing your baked goods with just a few tablespoons. This indispensable pantry staple is available in a range of varieties. It's important to understand the different characteristics of each in order to create the right texture, flavor, and appearance in your recipes.

Natural Cocoa Powder

Also known as unsweetened cocoa powder, natural cocoa powder is the purest form of cocoa powder, made by roasting, grinding, and pressing cocoa beans to remove most of the cocoa butter. It has a light brown, reddish hue and a fruity, bitter flavor. Because of its intense chocolate flavor and slightly acidic pH level, recipes with natural cocoa powder often use baking soda as the leavening agent since baking soda is alkaline and neutralizes the cocoa's acidity.

Dutch-Process Cocoa Powder

Dutch-process cocoa powder is treated with an alkalizing agent to neutralize its natural acidity, resulting in a milder, smoother flavor and a darker hue. Recipes with Dutch-process cocoa powder, which has a pH level closer to neutral, call for baking powder as the leavening agent to ensure the correct rise and texture. Due to its mellow and well-rounded chocolate flavor, it is typically my first choice to bake with. Most recipes in this book that feature cocoa powder use Dutch-process cocoa powder.

Black Cocoa Powder

Black cocoa powder is an ultra–Dutch-process cocoa powder, which means it has been alkalized to an even greater extent. This imparts an almost black color and a very low acidity level. It's most commonly used to achieve that iconic Oreo taste and color. While it adds a dramatic appearance and unique taste to desserts, black cocoa powder should be used sparingly, often in combination with unsweetened or Dutch-process cocoa to avoid creating a dry or crumbly texture.

CHOPPED CHOCOLATE BARS VS. CHOCOLATE CHIPS

Opting for chopped chocolate bars instead of chocolate chips in baking can make a significant difference in the final outcome of your dessert. Chocolate chips often contain fillers. This is why they maintain their shape in chocolate chip cookies, but the fillers can impact the chips' melting properties and lead to a grainy texture in your baked goods. As a result, I solely use chocolate chips as add-ins for cookies, bars, muffins, and quick breads.

When it comes to melted chocolate, use chopped chocolate bars or couverture chocolate to ensure a smoother, more consistent melt and a superior texture in your recipes. In addition, chocolate bars and couverture chocolate have a richer, more straightforward chocolate flavor that is better suited for cakes, fillings, and frostings. Ghirardelli makes an affordably priced chocolate bar that melts beautifully. I've also had great success with Valrhona, Lindt, Callebaut, and Cocoa Barry.

White chocolate can be especially finicky to work with due to its unique properties. White chocolate chips often have a low cocoa butter content (or none at all), which can lead to a grainy texture or cause the emulsion to split. To ensure a silky, creamy texture in your desserts, opt for high-quality white chocolate brands with a higher cocoa butter content, such as Valrhona, Callebaut, Cocoa Barry, or Green and Blacks. These premium options will deliver the desired consistency and elevate your chocolate creations.

MEASURING CHOCOLATE BARS VS. CHOCOLATE CHIPS

In this cookbook, you'll notice that chocolate measurements are provided in two different ways: ounces for chopped chocolate and cups for chocolate chips (rest assured, the grams equivalent is provided for both). The reason for this distinction is to ensure accuracy in your recipes and make it easier for you to work with these two types of chocolate.

Using ounces for chocolate bars aligns with the way they are packaged and labeled, making it simpler and more convenient for you to measure the correct amount.

Using dry measuring cups for chocolate chips allows you to easily scoop and level off the desired amount of chocolate chips.

By following these guidelines for measuring chocolate, you can ensure that your desserts turn out just as intended, with the perfect balance of chocolatey goodness.

QUICK CONVERSIONS FOR CHOCOLATE
1 CUP = 170 G (6 OZ)
¾ CUP = 130 G (4.5 OZ)
⅔ CUP = 115 G (4 OZ)
½ CUP = 85 G (3 OZ)
⅓ CUP = 57 G (2 OZ)
¼ CUP = 45 G (1.5 OZ)

TIPS FOR WORKING WITH CHOCOLATE

Baking is both an art and a science, and working with chocolate is no exception. In this section, you'll learn the nuances of melting chocolate, how to unlock the potential of cocoa, how to make a silky smooth ganache, how to caramelize white chocolate, and how to infuse flavors into your desserts. Understanding the insights and methods provided will elevate your chocolate endeavors to new heights and ensure each recipe you try is nothing short of perfection.

HOW TO MELT CHOCOLATE

Melting chocolate is a fundamental skill when baking with chocolate, as it ensures a smooth and even consistency in your recipes. There are two popular methods for melting chocolate: the double-boiler method and the microwave method. Follow these steps to achieve perfectly melted chocolate every time.

Double-Boiler Method
This classic technique involves gently melting chocolate using indirect heat to prevent scorching.

DIRECTIONS

1 Chop the chocolate into small, even pieces to ensure uniform melting. The finer the chop, the easier to melt.

2 Fill a saucepan with about 1 in [2.5 cm] of water and bring it to a gentle simmer over medium heat.

3 Place a heatproof bowl (glass or stainless steel) over the saucepan, making sure the bottom of the bowl does not touch the water.

4 Lower the heat to low and add the chopped chocolate to the bowl. Let it melt slowly, stirring occasionally with a rubber spatula to ensure even melting.

5 Once the chocolate has melted and become smooth, remove the bowl from the heat and carefully dry the underside of the bowl to avoid any water droplets coming into contact with the chocolate.

Chocolate is a diverse and delicate ingredient, and it can be temperamental to work with. Two important rules to know: 1. chocolate doesn't like high heat, and 2. chocolate doesn't like water or humidity. Here are a couple general tips to follow when melting chocolate:

- Always ensure your bowls, utensils, and work surfaces are completely dry before melting chocolate, as even a tiny amount of water can cause the chocolate to seize, becoming grainy and unusable.

- To prevent overheating, especially with the microwave method, be patient and melt the chocolate gradually using low heat settings and regular stirring. This will prevent the chocolate from burning or separating.

- Once melted, avoid shocking the chocolate by adding cold flavorings or ingredients. Sudden temperature changes can result in the chocolate instantly seizing and turning into a hard, solid lump. It's always best to use room-temperature or warm ingredients when working with melted chocolate.

Microwave Method
This quicker method is convenient for melting chocolate in small quantities, but it requires extra care to avoid overheating.

DIRECTIONS

1 Chop the chocolate into small, even pieces for uniform melting.

2 Place the chocolate in a microwave-safe bowl and microwave in 30-second intervals at a low heat setting, stirring after each interval.

3 Continue this process until the chocolate is almost completely melted, then remove it from the microwave and stir until it becomes smooth and fully melted. The residual heat will help melt any remaining small pieces.

BLOOMING COCOA POWDER

As you work your way through this cookbook, you'll find that some recipes call for "blooming" cocoa powder. This method involves mixing cocoa powder with a hot liquid such as hot water, coffee, tea, milk, oil, or melted butter to help activate the cocoa's flavors and unlock its full potential.

Cocoa powder is naturally acidic and can often have a metallic aftertaste, but when cocoa powder is bloomed, it dissolves and releases its deep, rich chocolatey taste, resulting in a more intense and well-rounded flavor. It's like a magic trick! Keep an eye out for this technique in the snacking cake and celebration cake chapters, and be sure to follow the instructions for blooming cocoa powder so you get the best possible results.

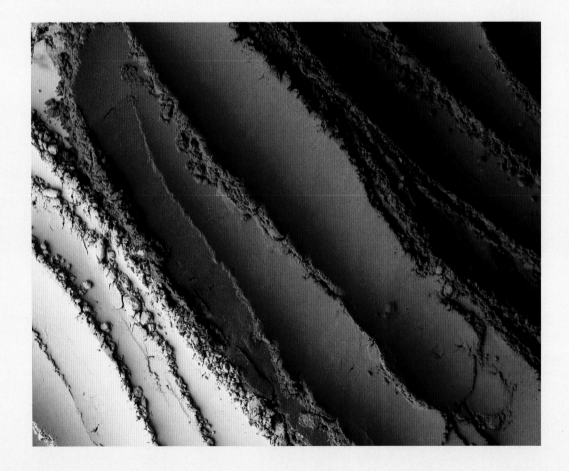

A GUIDE TO GANACHE

Ganache is a versatile, velvety mixture of chocolate and heavy cream, used as a glaze, filling, frosting, or even truffles. The key to creating the perfect ganache is understanding the appropriate ratio of heavy cream to chocolate, which varies depending on the type of chocolate you're using and the desired consistency for your dessert. Different ingredients, such as butter and eggs, can also be used to make ganache, but the most common ganache type is heavy cream–based. Here's a quick overview of how to make it.

DIRECTIONS

1 **Chop the Chocolate:** Start by finely chopping your chosen chocolate (white, milk, semisweet, or dark) into small, even pieces to ensure it melts uniformly when mixed with the hot cream. Place the chopped chocolate in a heatproof bowl.

2 **Heat the Heavy Cream:** Pour the heavy cream into a saucepan and heat it over medium heat until it begins to steam and small bubbles form around the edges—a gentle simmer. Do not let the cream come to a full rolling boil.

3 **Combine the Chocolate and Cream:** Pour the hot cream over the chopped chocolate. Let the mixture sit for a minute or two, undisturbed, allowing the chocolate to soften. Then, gently stir the mixture with a whisk or spatula until the chocolate has fully melted and the ganache is smooth. For a silky texture, use an immersion blender.

4 **Cool and Use the Ganache:** Allow the ganache to cool until it reaches the desired consistency for your dessert. For a glaze or pourable filling, use the ganache while it's still warm and fluid. For frosting or whipped ganache, let it cool completely and then whip with an electric mixer until light and fluffy. Store ganache in an airtight container in the fridge for up to 2 weeks.

HOW TO CARAMELIZE WHITE CHOCOLATE

Caramelized white chocolate is a delightful twist on traditional white chocolate, characterized by an irresistibly rich, toasty flavor and a beautiful golden hue. The caramelization process involves heating white chocolate at a low temperature, allowing the sugar to slowly caramelize, which transforms the taste and color. It is essential to use high-quality white chocolate that contains at least 30% cocoa butter in this method, otherwise the chocolate will seize and become grainy. I've had great success with Valrhona and Green and Black brands. Follow these steps to caramelize white chocolate, which you can use to add an extra layer of deliciousness to your favorite recipes, such as White Chocolate Macadamia Nut Cookies (page 47), Espresso Chocolate Rye Sablés (page 65), or Chocolate Stout Rye Bundt (page 125). (If you don't have time to make it yourself, you can also find prepackaged caramelized white chocolate, like Valrhona Dulcey.)

DIRECTIONS

1 **Preheat the Oven:** Begin by preheating the oven to 250°F [120°C]. This low temperature will allow the white chocolate to caramelize slowly and evenly.

2 **Prepare the Chocolate:** Chop your high-quality white chocolate bars into small, evenly sized pieces to ensure uniform melting. Line a rimmed baking sheet with parchment paper or a silicone baking mat. Spread the chopped white chocolate in an even layer across the prepared baking sheet.

3 **Caramelize in the Oven:** Place the baking sheet in the preheated oven and bake for 10 minutes. After 10 minutes, use a rubber spatula to stir and redistribute the white chocolate. Return the baking sheet to the oven and repeat this process every 10 minutes until the chocolate reaches a deep, golden caramel color. This may take anywhere from 30 to 60 minutes, depending on the chocolate and your oven.

4 **Cool and Store:** Once the white chocolate has reached the desired caramelization level, remove it from the oven and allow it to cool completely on the baking sheet. The caramelized white chocolate will become firm as it cools. Break or chop it into smaller pieces for use in your recipes, or store it in an airtight container at room temperature for up to 1 month.

INFUSING HEAVY CREAM:
THE SECRET TO ADDING FLAVOR

Infusing heavy cream with flavors like tea or coffee can elevate your desserts to new heights. Experiment with different tea blends, coffee roasts, or other aromatic ingredients to discover unique and delicious flavor combinations. Use infused cream as an ingredient to add layers of complexity and depth, like the banana milk in the Chocolate Banana Cream Pie (page 165) or the coffee cream in the Coffee Caramel Nutella Tart (page 155), or as a luxurious topping to finish off a dish, like the malted whipped cream in the Chocolate Malt Cream Pie (page 159). It's a simple process—here's how to do it.

DIRECTIONS

1 **Heat the Cream:** Pour the heavy cream into a saucepan and heat it over medium-low heat until it's steaming but not boiling. It should reach a temperature of about 175°F [80°C] for optimal infusion.

2 **Add a Flavoring Agent:** Once the cream is heated, turn off the heat and add your chosen flavoring agents (tea leaves, coffee grounds, vanilla beans, malted milk powder, herbs, spices, etc.) to the saucepan, stirring gently to ensure even distribution. If the flavoring agent dissolves and doesn't need to be strained, which will happen with espresso powder or malted milk powder, then there's no need to steep and you can use right away.

3 **Steep and Infuse:** Cover the saucepan with a tight-fitting lid and let the cream steep for 10 minutes.

4 **Strain and Cool:** After the infusion is complete, remove the plastic wrap and strain the cream through a fine-mesh sieve or cheesecloth into a clean bowl to remove the flavoring agents. Use right away as the recipe states or, if making in advance or using as whipped cream, allow the cream to cool to room temperature, then cover and refrigerate until needed.

5 **Whip:** Once your infused cream is chilled, you can whisk it in a stand mixer or using a hand mixer to create flavored whipped cream for a decadent topping or filling.

TIPS FOR SUCCESS

Read the recipe first

Before diving into any recipe, it's essential to read it thoroughly from start to finish. This not only familiarizes you with the steps and required ingredients but also helps you plan your time effectively. By understanding the recipe, you can anticipate potential challenges and avoid surprises, ensuring a smoother baking experience.

Practice mise en place

Mise en place is a French term that translates to "everything in its place." In the context of baking, it means gathering and preparing all the necessary ingredients before you begin. This includes measuring, chopping, and mixing the ingredients as required. Practicing mise en place streamlines the baking process, reduces stress, and helps prevent errors, such as leaving out a crucial ingredient or misreading a step in the recipe.

Use a scale to measure ingredients

Precision is key when it comes to baking, and using a kitchen scale ensures accuracy. Scales provide a more consistent and reliable result than measuring cups or spoons, as they account for variations in ingredient density and packing. By measuring ingredients by weight, you'll boost your chances of success. Plus, it's less messy and uses fewer dishes! I've provided weight measurements for both dry and liquid ingredients in all the recipes.

Measure your flour correctly

If you don't have a scale, the spoon-and-level method is the next best approach for measuring flour accurately. To do this, use a spoon to lightly scoop flour into a measuring cup until it's overflowing. Do not tap or shake the cup. Then, use a straight-edged utensil, like the back of a knife, to level off the excess flour. Avoid scooping the flour directly out of the flour bag or bin, as this will compact the flour and lead to an inaccurate measurement. In this book, 1 cup of flour equals 125 grams.

Use liquid measuring cups

If you don't have a scale, when measuring liquids (such as milk, buttermilk, coffee, sour cream, oil, mascarpone, or crème fraîche), use a liquid measuring cup, such as a glass Pyrex, instead of a standard dry measuring cup. Liquid measuring cups are designed with clear markings and a spout for easy pouring, ensuring accurate and mess-free measurements. Unlike a measuring cup used for dry ingredients like flour, liquid measuring cups allow you to top off the liquids to the line without spilling. To measure liquids correctly, place the cup on a level surface and pour in the liquid until it reaches the desired mark when looking at eye-level.

Be a bowl scraper

Whenever you're using a stand mixer, it's important to regularly scrape down the sides and bottom of the bowl as well as the paddle, where butter or dry patches of flour can easily get stuck. Scrape the bowl and paddle after each addition of new ingredients to ensure everything is well combined and incorporated.

A well-stocked pantry ensures you always have the necessary ingredients whenever a chocolate craving strikes. The following is a comprehensive list of ingredients I've used in this book. Included are essential pantry staples and specialty baking ingredients, which can be found at your local grocery store or ordered online. I've also highlighted my personal favorite brands that have been instrumental in developing these recipes.

CHOCOLATE AND COCOA POWDER

Black Cocoa Powder

Black cocoa powder imparts a deep, rich color to your baked goods while providing that signature Oreo-like taste. I buy my black cocoa online from King Arthur Baking Company, as it has an ultra-dark, intense flavor.

Caramelized White Chocolate

For a convenient and delicious caramelized white chocolate option, I recommend Valrhona's Dulcey chocolate. This high-quality product saves you time by eliminating the need to make caramelized white chocolate from scratch and provides a delectable, rich flavor and smooth texture. If you can't get store-bought caramelized white chocolate, you can make your own following the steps on page 18.

Chocolate Bars

For the best flavor and texture, I recommend using high-quality chocolate bars such as Ghirardelli, Valrhona, Guittard, or Lindt. These brands offer a superior taste that will elevate your creations to new heights.

Chocolate Chips

While chocolate chips are convenient, most recipes in this book call for chopped chocolate bars, as chocolate chips often contain fillers that can affect the texture and flavor of your desserts. For recipes that do call for chocolate chips, I like using Ghirardelli, Guittard, or Nestlé brand chocolate chips.

Couverture Chocolate

Couverture chocolate is a premium-quality chocolate with a higher percentage of cocoa butter. It is ground to a finer texture than regular chocolate, making it ideal for tempering, coating, and melting. Its smooth texture and superior flavor make it a preferred choice among pastry chefs and chocolatiers. You can use couverture chocolate interchangeably with chocolate chips or chocolate bars. My favorite brands are Valrhona, Callebaut, Cacao Barry, and Guittard. You can buy directly from these companies' websites or through other online retailers such as World Wide Chocolate.

Dutch-Process Cocoa Powder

My go-to choice for Dutch-process cocoa powder is Valrhona, as it delivers the best taste and flavor. This is the most widely used brand in bakeries across the world. However, Hershey's Special Dark, Guittard Rouge, and Ghirardelli Dutch-Process cocoa are other excellent, more accessible at-home options that you can find at any grocery store. Most recipes in this cookbook utilize Dutch-process cocoa powder for its optimal flavor and rich, velvety texture.

EGGS AND DAIRY

Butter
Use unsalted butter unless otherwise specified. This allows you to control the salt content in your recipes, ensuring a perfect balance between sweet and savory flavors.

Cream Cheese
For a rich and creamy texture, I recommend using Philadelphia Cream Cheese. This brand offers a consistently high-quality product that enhances the overall taste and mouthfeel of your baked goods.

Crème Fraîche
This tangy and velvety ingredient adds a luxurious touch to your recipe. I like using Vermont Creamery.

Eggs
Large eggs are the standard size used in these recipes, with each egg weighing around 55 grams. Eggs provide structure, moisture, and richness to your baked goods, contributing to their overall texture and taste.

Heavy Cream
I prefer using the Horizon Organic brand of heavy cream in my recipes. This high-quality cream contains no fillers, providing a smooth and creamy consistency to ganaches, frostings, and whipped cream.

Mascarpone
An Italian cream cheese, mascarpone offers a silky-smooth texture and a mild, slightly sweet flavor that complements chocolate beautifully.

Milk
All recipes in this cookbook call for whole milk. Don't skimp on the fat when it comes to dairy! The higher fat content yields optimal flavor and texture.

Ricotta
For the best results, choose whole-milk ricotta. This ingredient provides a delicate yet creamy texture to your desserts. Be sure to strain it thoroughly before using to ensure a smooth and even consistency.

Sour Cream
I recommend using Daisy brand sour cream for its rich and tangy flavor that balances out the sweetness in your baked goods. Use whole-fat for the best results.

EXTRACTS

Vanilla Extract
To achieve an authentic and rich vanilla flavor in your desserts, use real vanilla extract, as it imparts a depth and complexity that imitation products cannot match.

Vanilla Bean Paste
Nielsen-Massey Vanillas' vanilla bean paste is a favorite of mine, as it contains real vanilla seeds, providing an intense flavor and beautiful flecks of vanilla throughout your desserts. This concentrated paste is a fantastic way to elevate the taste and appearance of your chocolate creations. You can substitute vanilla bean paste 1:1 in place of vanilla extract.

FATS, OILS, AND PASTES

Miso
The recipes in this book use only white (shiro) miso. This variety is lighter than other miso pastes and provides a subtle, savory depth that complements sweet flavors beautifully in baking.

Neutral Oil
When a recipe calls for a neutral oil, use light-flavored options like canola or vegetable oil. These oils provide moisture and a tender crumb to your baked goods without interfering with or overpowering the flavor.

Olive Oil
Use a high-quality olive oil for the best results and flavor. A good olive oil will provide a subtle fruity note and enhance the overall taste of your creations without overpowering the chocolate.

Peanut Butter
For the best texture and consistency, I recommend using Skippy or JIF peanut butter. Avoid substituting with natural peanut butter, as it tends to be oily and has a thinner consistency that may not yield the desired results.

Tahini
For a rich and creamy tahini, I recommend Soom Foods brand. Its high-quality product has a smooth texture and nutty flavor that pairs wonderfully with chocolate. Remember to stir the tahini well before using to ensure even consistency and flavor distribution in your desserts.

FLOURS

All-Purpose Flour
For consistent results in baked goods, my favorite all-purpose flour brands are King Arthur, Bob's Red Mill, and Trader Joe's. I recommend using unbleached flour. If you don't have a scale, remember to use the spoon-and-level method (see page 20) when measuring to ensure accuracy.

Almond Flour
For recipes that call for almond flour, I prefer using blanched almond flour. It has a fine texture and delicate flavor that pairs wonderfully with chocolate, adding a tender crumb to your baked goods.

Bread Flour
For recipes that require a bit more structure and elasticity, bread flour is the perfect choice. It has a higher protein content compared to all-purpose flour, which helps create a stronger gluten network, resulting in a chewier texture and improved crumb structure in your baked goods. I recommend King Arthur's bread flour.

Buckwheat Flour
Buckwheat lends an earthy, nutty flavor that pairs so well with chocolate. I like using Bob's Red Mill or Arrowhead Mills brands. Both can be found at grocery stores like Sprouts or Whole Foods or can be purchased online.

Cake Flour
When it comes to creating a light and tender crumb, cake flour is your best friend. Its lower protein content compared to all-purpose flour ensures that your cakes remain delicate and airy. If you find yourself without cake flour, don't worry! You can easily replicate its effects by measuring out 1 cup [125 g] of all-purpose flour, then replacing 2 Tbsp of the flour with cornstarch. This substitution will

help mimic the lower protein content of cake flour, resulting in a similarly tender and light texture in your chocolate creations.

Dark Rye Flour

When it comes to dark rye flour, I recommend Bob's Red Mill brand. It's finely ground, which ensures a smooth texture in your baked goods. The rich, earthy flavor of dark rye flour complements chocolate desserts perfectly, adding depth and complexity to their taste.

LEAVENERS

Baking Powder

I recommend using non-aluminum, double-acting baking powder for consistent rise and a neutral taste in your desserts.

Baking Soda

This leavening agent is activated by acidic ingredients like buttermilk, creating a tender and airy crumb in your baked goods.

Cream of Tartar

Cream of tartar, also known as potassium bitartrate, is derived from tartaric acid and is a byproduct of winemaking. Due to its acidic properties, it is commonly used in baking to stabilize egg whites in meringues, prevent sugar from crystallizing in syrups and confections, and act as a leavening agent to enhance the texture of your baked goods.

SPICES, POWDERS, AND THICKENING AGENTS

Cornstarch

Cornstarch is a fine, powdery starch used as a thickening agent in cooking and baking, often to set sauces and puddings. Cornstarch is also used in baking to lighten and tenderize baked goods such as shortbread or cakes.

Espresso Powder

This ingredient adds depth and enhances the natural flavors of chocolate, creating a rich and complex taste profile in your finished desserts.

Flaky Sea Salt

Maldon flaky sea salt is my go-to finishing salt for chocolate cookies and other sweet treats. The delicate, pyramid-shaped crystals add a satisfying crunch and a burst of saltiness to sweet treats.

Gelatin

When it comes to stabilizing and setting your fillings, Knox powdered gelatin is my top choice. This reliable and widely available product provides consistent results, ensuring that your fillings and creams hold their shape and maintain a silky texture. To use Knox powdered gelatin, follow the specific instructions provided in each recipe, as the amount and method of hydration may vary.

Kosher Salt

My preferred brand of kosher salt is Diamond Crystal. Its consistent granule size and pure taste make it an excellent choice for balancing and enhancing the flavors in your chocolate desserts. If using Morton kosher salt, use scant teaspoons, as it has a larger crystal size and a saltier taste.

Malted Milk Powder

My preferred brand of malted milk powder is King Arthur, which delivers a consistent and delicious result. Nestlé's malted milk powder is another great option that is readily available at most grocery stores.

Brown Sugar

The rich molasses flavor of brown sugar results in caramelized notes in your baked goods. My go-to brand is C&H brown sugar. The recipes in this book specify which type, but light and dark brown sugar can be used interchangeably.

Confectioners' Sugar

Also known as powdered sugar or icing sugar, confectioners' sugar is a fine, powdery sugar perfect for dusting and glazes. Be sure to sift before using to remove any clumps and ensure a smooth finish.

Demerara Sugar

Demerara sugar is a type of raw sugar with a coarse texture and large, golden crystals, originating from the Demerara region of Guyana, where it was first produced. It's minimally refined and contains traces of molasses, which gives it a distinct toffee-like flavor. It's commonly used as a finishing sugar to add a crunchy texture to baked goods or to sweeten beverages such as coffee and tea. Though slightly different from turbinado in texture and taste, demerara can be swapped with it in recipes.

Granulated Sugar

Granulated sugar is a versatile and essential ingredient in many dessert recipes. Its neutral sweetness helps balance and showcase the rich flavors of chocolate creations in particular. I use C&H Sugar or just the regular store brand.

Light Corn Syrup

When a recipe calls for light corn syrup, do not substitute dark corn syrup, as they will yield different results. The darker variety has a more robust flavor and darker color that may overpower your dessert.

Maple Syrup

When baking, it's essential to use real maple syrup for both flavor and consistency. Pure maple syrup has a distinct, rich, and complex sweetness that cannot be replicated by artificial alternatives. So, when possible, opt for the real deal.

Turbinado Sugar

Sometimes known as raw sugar or sugar in the raw, turbinado has large, golden crystals and a mild caramel flavor. It lends a delightful crunch and subtle sweetness to your chocolate treats and is a great finishing sugar.

TOOLS AND EQUIPMENT

Whether you're a beginner baker or a seasoned pro, having the right tools and equipment is essential for successful baking and can greatly improve your baking experience. Here you'll find everything from must-have tools you'll reach for every time you bake to specialized equipment you might want to add to your wish list.

Baking Sheets
I recommend using heavy-duty, light-colored baking sheets, such as those from Nordic Ware. They are durable, are less prone to warping, and last a long time.

Bench Scraper
A versatile tool for handling bread or pie dough, shaping edges, and creating beautiful chocolate curls. It's also great for portioning and transferring ingredients.

Candy Thermometer
This specialized thermometer is crucial for accurately measuring temperatures when deep frying or making caramel or other sugar-based confections.

Cookie Scoop
A reliable cookie scoop, like the Vollrath 1 oz scoop, ensures evenly sized cookies for consistent baking results.

Digital Thermometer
A high-quality digital thermometer, like the Thermapen, is essential for checking the temperature of pastry creams or fillings and testing the doneness of cakes or breads.

Dry Measuring Cups and Spoons
Essential for accurately measuring dry ingredients like flour, cocoa powder, and sugar.

Electric Hand Mixer
A convenient and portable option for simpler recipes that don't require a stand mixer.

Electric Stand Mixer
A powerful and versatile kitchen appliance, my KitchenAid stand mixer is a workhorse in my kitchen. I recommend the Artisan 5 Quart Tilt-Head Stand Mixer for everyday baking and the Professional Series for making bread.

Food Processor
A versatile kitchen appliance that can chop, blend, shred, and purée ingredients, making it useful for recipes that call for finely chopped nuts or smooth purées, like the Creamy Chocolate Cheesecake Bars (page 93).

Immersion Blender
This handheld blender allows you to effortlessly make silky smooth ganaches, sauces, or pastry creams.

Kitchen Scale
I cannot emphasize this enough: A kitchen scale is an essential tool for every baker. It ensures accuracy, precision, and efficiency in prepping ingredients, making your baking experience smoother and more enjoyable. I use the Escali brand scale, which is affordable and can be purchased online on Amazon.

Kitchen Scissors
Handy for cutting parchment paper to line baking pans or cake pans or trimming dough edges.

Liquid Measuring Cups
Use glass or plastic measuring cups, like Pyrex, for liquids such as milk, oil, and sour cream.

Offset Spatula
Ideal for smoothing the top of batters, leveling ingredients in pans, and decorating cakes. The angled design allows for better control and even spreading.

Parchment Paper
This nonstick surface is perfect for lining baking sheets and pans, making cleanup a breeze, and preventing your baked goods from sticking.

Pastry Bags
I prefer disposable pastry bags for easy cleanup. They're perfect for piping and decorating your cakes and tarts.

Pastry Brush
Useful for removing excess flour or crumbs from surfaces, applying glazes or washes, and brushing off excess ingredients.

Pastry Tips
These come in various shapes and sizes for different piping effects. I specify the appropriate tip for each recipe in this book.

Pizza Cutter
An excellent tool for trimming or cutting through doughs quickly and easily. Its sharp wheel ensures clean, precise cuts while reducing the chances of tearing or distorting the dough.

Rolling Pin
An indispensable tool for rolling out dough for pies, cookies, and pastries. Choose one that feels comfortable in your hands.

Rubber Spatula
Rubber spatulas are heat resistant and great for scraping bowls, folding ingredients, and stirring mixtures. My brand of choice is Vollrath for its heavy-duty, high-heat capabilities.

Ruler
A simple but useful tool for measuring dough thickness and dimensions.

Sifter
A must-have for sifting cocoa and confectioners' sugar, ensuring a smooth, lump-free texture in your desserts.

Silicone Baking Mat
Silpat brand mats or similar alternatives provide a reusable nonstick surface. I use silicone baking mats for cooling caramels or candies like toffee.

Silicone Pastry Brush
I prefer to use this for applying egg washes, as it is easy to clean and won't retain odors or flavors.

Skewers or Chopsticks
Perfect for swirling batters, creating marbled effects, or testing the doneness of baked goods.

Toothpick
Use this simple tool to check the doneness of baked goods by inserting it into the center and checking for crumbs or wet batter.

Wire Rack
An essential tool for allowing your baked goods to cool properly.

Wire Whisk
Useful for incorporating air into ingredients, blending mixtures, and preventing lumps in batters or sauces.

Zester
I use a Microplane for zesting citrus fruits and grating chocolate finely.

SWEET TREATS

N° 1

CHOCOLATE LOVER

BLISSFUL / BITES

Strawberry Matcha White Chocolate Bark	33
Brown Butter–Chocolate Crispy Treats	35
Malted Hot Cocoa Mix	37
Peanut Pretzel Toffee Bark	39
Nama Chocolate Ganache Truffles	41

STRAWBERRY MATCHA WHITE CHOCOLATE BARK

MAKES 1¼ LB [570 G]	
Two 10 oz bags [570 g total]	white coating chocolate
1 Tbsp	culinary-grade matcha powder
½ cup [8 g]	freeze-dried strawberries, chopped

If you're looking for a fun and easy way to get creative in the kitchen with your kiddos, chocolate bark is the answer. It uses just a few pantry ingredients and requires minimal prep time. I love using coating chocolate as a shortcut because there's no need to temper the chocolate. This Strawberry Matcha White Chocolate Bark is my personal favorite, but the Crunch Bark and Cookies and Cream variations are close runners-up. Feel free to swap in your favorite nuts, cereal, cookies, candies, dried fruit, or salty snacks to make it your own or to match the occasion.

DIRECTIONS

1   Line a baking sheet with parchment paper. In a large heatproof bowl, add the coating chocolate and melt over a double boiler (see page 14). Once melted, remove from the heat.

2   In a separate small bowl, spoon out 8 oz [225 g] of the melted white chocolate and set aside. It doesn't have to be precise! This will be used to create the decorative swirls.

3   To the large bowl, sift in the matcha powder and stir until combined. Using an offset spatula, spread the matcha chocolate in an even layer onto the prepared baking sheet.

4   Carefully spoon dollops of white chocolate over the matcha layer and use a toothpick to make swirls. Sprinkle the top with freeze-dried strawberries in an even layer.

5   Let the bark set at room temperature until fully cooled, or put in the refrigerator to speed up the cooling process. Break the bark into pieces and store in an airtight container in the refrigerator for up to 2 weeks.

VARIATIONS

Crunch Bark: Combine 10 oz [285 g] melted dark coating chocolate with 1 cup [30 g] Rice Krispies cereal and stir until combined. Transfer to a parchment paper–lined baking tray and spread into an even layer using the back of a rubber spatula or offset spatula. Sprinkle with flaky sea salt if you like. Chill in the refrigerator for 15 minutes or until set.

Cookies and Cream Bark: Finely chop ten whole Oreo cookies (with the filling) and sift to remove the fine cookie dust. Combine the chopped cookies with 10 oz [285 g] melted white chocolate and stir until combined. Transfer to a parchment paper–lined baking tray and spread into an even layer using the back of a rubber spatula or offset spatula. Chill in the refrigerator for 15 minutes or until set.

BROWN BUTTER—CHOCOLATE CRISPY TREATS

MAKES 16 LARGE OR 24 SMALL TREATS	
1 cup [225 g]	unsalted butter, cubed
Two 10 oz bags [570 g total]	mini marshmallows, divided
2 Tbsp	unsweetened natural cocoa powder
½ tsp	kosher salt
½ tsp	vanilla bean paste or extract
15½ oz [440 g]	Cocoa Krispies cereal (about 10½ cups)
¾ cup [130 g]	mini semisweet chocolate chips, divided
Flaky sea salt, for sprinkling (optional)	

I think it's fair to say that rice crispy treats are the true embodiment of nostalgia. Such humble ingredients can yield a crispy, gooey, buttery masterpiece. For this recipe, I made a few tweaks to the create a chocolate lover's version. The brown butter, salt, and cocoa powder elevate these simple treats to the next level. I also like to hold back some mini marshmallows to add at the end so there are surprising pops of marshmallows throughout. Although this recipe is a bit more involved than the original, everything comes together quickly.

DIRECTIONS

1 Grease a 9 by 13 in [23 by 33 cm] baking dish with nonstick spray. Set aside 2 cups [115 g] of mini marshmallows.

2 In a large pot over medium heat, melt the butter, stirring frequently with a rubber spatula. Brown the butter until it turns a golden amber color and gives off a nutty aroma, 5 to 7 minutes. Be patient and keep an eye on it.

3 Once the butter is browned, immediately remove from the heat and add the remaining marshmallows, cocoa powder, salt, and vanilla. Stir with a rubber spatula until fully incorporated. If the residual heat is not enough to fully melt the marshmallows, return the pot to low heat and stir until the mixture is smooth.

4 As soon as the marshmallows are completely melted, remove the pot from

the heat and add the cereal. Gently stir to coat evenly. Add in ½ cup [85 g] of the mini chocolate chips and the reserved 2 cups [115 g] of marshmallows and stir to distribute evenly.

5 Spread the mixture into the prepared pan in an even layer. Top with the remaining ¼ cup [43 g] mini chocolate chips and sprinkle with flaky sea salt, if using. Let cool for 1 hour. Cut into 16 large squares or 24 small squares and serve. Store the treats in an airtight container at room temperature for up to 2 days.

VARIATIONS

PB Chocolate Treats: Add 2 Tbsp of creamy peanut butter (not the natural kind) to the melted marshmallow mixture.

Bourbon Chocolate Treats: Add 1 Tbsp of bourbon to the melted marshmallow mixture.

MALTED HOT COCOA MIX

MAKES 12 SERVINGS	
8 oz [225 g]	dark chocolate
1 cup [85 g]	unsweetened natural cocoa powder
½ cup [45 g]	nonfat dry milk powder
1 cup [200 g]	granulated sugar
1 cup [120 g]	malted milk powder
4 tsp	cornstarch
½ tsp	kosher salt

The second the weather starts to cool down, a warm mug of hot chocolate is a must. When I was a kid, I was addicted to those Swiss Miss hot chocolate packets—specifically the ones with mini marshmallows. Topped with whipped cream, it was always a treat. But why settle for store-bought packets when you can easily make your own mix at home? To make this mix extra special, I use toasted milk powder to add an extra caramelized flavor and finely ground quality chocolate in addition to the cocoa powder for extra indulgence. Make a double batch with the kiddos and keep a jar of this mix on hand all winter long.

DIRECTIONS

1   In a small food processor, combine the chocolate and cocoa powder and process into a powder.

2   In a small skillet over medium heat, toast the milk powder, stirring frequently with a rubber spatula until golden brown, about 5 minutes. Transfer to a mixing bowl and let cool completely. Add the chocolate mixture and the sugar, malted milk powder, cornstarch, and salt and whisk to combine. Store the cocoa mix in a large Mason jar or airtight container for up to 1 month.

3   For one serving of hot cocoa, heat 1 cup [240 g] of milk in a small saucepan over medium heat just until it starts to steam and small bubbles appear around the edge. Stir in ¼ cup [40 g] of the hot cocoa mix and, whisking constantly, continue to heat until it reaches a simmer. Pour the hot chocolate into a mug and top with mini marshmallows and whipped cream, if desired.

PEANUT PRETZEL TOFFEE BARK

MAKES 1½ LB [680 G]	
¾ cup [105 g]	salted roasted peanuts
1 cup [225 g]	unsalted butter, cubed
1 cup [200 g]	granulated sugar
1 Tbsp	light corn syrup
1 tsp	vanilla extract
½ tsp	kosher salt
½ tsp	baking soda
6 oz [170 g]	semisweet or dark chocolate, chopped
¾ cup [30 g]	pretzels, chopped (see Note)

NOTE ○ For a neat appearance, strain the super-fine pretzel dust from the chopped pretzels and discard, leaving only the chopped pretzel pieces.

Every Christmas season, my mom would buy boxes of assorted See's Candies chocolates for family and friends. I now carry on that tradition by making my own homemade toffee and giving it as a thoughtful hostess gift or sweet party favor for guests, because nothing says *I love you* like buttery toffee. This classic candy is surprisingly easy to make, and I've perfected the recipe with a few tips and tricks. A touch of corn syrup adds extra insurance to prevent the sugar syrup from crystallizing; baking soda gives the toffee a delicate texture; and cooking the toffee to a higher temperature ensures a nice snap and crunch that won't stick to your teeth.

DIRECTIONS

1 Chop the peanuts and set aside. Line a baking sheet with a silicone baking mat.

2 In a large saucepan fitted with a candy thermometer, combine the butter, sugar, 2 Tbsp of water, and the corn syrup. Bring to a boil over medium-low heat, stirring often with a rubber spatula. Once the sugar syrup reaches about 225°F [107°C], stir in the peanuts.

3 Turn the heat down to low and cook the sugar mixture, stirring constantly, until it achieves a dark amber color and reaches 310°F [154°C], 15 to 20 minutes. Be patient and don't rush the process!

4 Remove from the heat quickly, add the vanilla, salt, and baking soda, and mix thoroughly.

5 Pour the toffee onto the prepared baking sheet and, using an offset spatula, spread into an even layer before the toffee sets. Immediately sprinkle the chopped chocolate over the hot toffee and allow it to soften and melt, undisturbed, for about 2 minutes. Spread the melted chocolate into an even layer across the toffee and immediately sprinkle the chopped pretzels all over the chocolate while it is still warm and melty. Gently press the pretzel pieces into the chocolate using your hands.

6 Let the toffee cool completely at room temperature. Once set, break the toffee apart into pieces. Store in an airtight container in a cool, dry place for up to 1 week or in the fridge for up to 2 weeks.

NAMA CHOCOLATE GANACHE TRUFFLES

MAKES 64 TRUFFLES	
1 lb [455 g]	60% dark chocolate, chopped
1½ cups [360 g]	heavy cream
2 Tbsp	light corn syrup or honey
¼ cup [57 g]	unsalted butter, cubed, at room temperature
Dutch-process cocoa powder, for dusting	

The term *nama* translates to "raw" or "fresh" in Japanese and refers to the fresh cream used to make this chocolate ganache. Nama chocolate was popularized by the Japanese luxury chocolate brand Royce. These chocolate confections are soft and velvety, with a texture that melts in your mouth. Despite their striking appearance, they are easy to make. The chocolate ganache comes together in just a few simple steps and is cut into neat squares—no scooping or rolling required. This makes for an easier, less messy process. Since there are only a few ingredients, using good-quality chocolate and butter is essential.

DIRECTIONS

1 Line an 8 in [20 cm] square baking pan with parchment paper, leaving an overhang on two sides.

2 Place the chopped chocolate into a large mixing bowl. Set aside.

3 In a small saucepan over medium heat, combine the heavy cream and corn syrup and bring to a boil. Pour the cream over the chopped chocolate and let sit, undisturbed, for 2 minutes. Starting from the center and working your way to the sides of the bowl, whisk until the mixture is smooth and emulsified.

4 Add the butter and whisk until smooth and the butter is fully incorporated. For a super silky texture, process with an immersion blender for a few seconds.

5 Pour the ganache into the prepared baking pan and smooth the top with an offset spatula, tilting the pan as needed. Tap the pan on the counter to remove any air bubbles and smooth again. Allow the ganache to cool slightly, then transfer to the refrigerator to set for 3 to 5 hours.

6 Once fully set, carefully remove the ganache from the baking pan. Cut into 1 in [2.5 cm] cubes, using a sharp knife dipped into hot water and wiped between each cut. Dust the tops with cocoa powder. Store in an airtight container in the fridge for up to 1 week.

CHEWY / GOOEY   N° 2

CHOCOLATE LOVER

COOKIES

STRAWBERRY AND CREAM COOKIES

MAKES 27 COOKIES	
2¾ cups [345 g]	all-purpose flour
1 tsp	kosher salt
½ tsp	cream of tartar
½ tsp	baking powder
½ tsp	baking soda
1 cup [225 g]	unsalted butter, at room temperature
1 cup [200 g]	light brown sugar, packed
1 cup [200 g]	granulated sugar, divided
1	large egg, at room temperature
1	large egg yolk, at room temperature
1 tsp	vanilla extract
2 cups [32 g]	freeze-dried strawberries, chopped
8 oz [225 g]	white chocolate chips or chopped white chocolate

These cookies are every bit as good as the name would suggest. They're my husband's favorite, and he lovingly describes them as having a taste of summer in every bite. Good news: You can have them all year round since they use freeze-dried strawberries instead of fresh. The freeze-dried strawberries add a refreshing hint of sweetness and a burst of flavor that goes so well with the creamy white chocolate chips. The cream of tartar enhances the brightness of the strawberries and yields a soft, chewy texture similar to a snickerdoodle.

DIRECTIONS

1   In a medium bowl, combine the flour, salt, cream of tartar, baking powder, and baking soda and set aside.

2   In the bowl of a stand mixer fitted with the paddle attachment, beat the butter, brown sugar, and ½ cup [100 g] of the granulated sugar on medium speed for 5 minutes, until light, fluffy, and pale in color. Add the egg and egg yolk one at a time until each is incorporated. Add the vanilla and beat on medium speed for another minute until fully combined. Scrape down the paddle and bowl.

3   Add the flour mixture and beat on low speed just until combined, about 30 seconds. Scrape down the bowl. Add the freeze-dried strawberries and white chocolate chips and mix on low speed to incorporate, 5 to 10 seconds. Place plastic wrap directly on the surface of the cookie dough and refrigerate for 1 hour to let all the ingredients get to know each other.

4   Adjust the oven rack to the middle position and preheat the oven to 350°F [175°C]. Line a baking sheet with parchment paper.   →

5   Put the remaining ½ cup [100 g] of granulated sugar in a small bowl. Scoop the cookie dough using a 1 oz cookie scoop. Roll each dough ball in the sugar and transfer to the prepared baking sheet. Bake for 10 to 12 minutes. For perfectly round cookies, use a large cookie cutter or wide glass (must be wider than the cookie) and gently swirl it in a circular motion around each warm cookie to shape the edges. Transfer the baking sheet to a wire rack and let the cookies cool completely before removing from the pan. Store the cookies in an airtight container at room temperature for up to 3 days.

TO FREEZE THE COOKIE DOUGH

Place the parchment paper–lined baking sheet with the scooped dough in the freezer for about 20 minutes, until the dough balls are set, then transfer the cookie dough to a plastic bag or freezer-safe container and stash for up to 1 month.

VARIATION

Matcha, Strawberry, and Cream Cookies:
Add 1 Tbsp of culinary-grade matcha powder to the flour mixture in step 1 for a matcha-strawberry version.

WHITE CHOCOLATE MACADAMIA NUT COOKIES

MAKES 28 COOKIES	
1 cup plus 3 Tbsp [268 g]	unsalted butter, cubed
2½ cups [315 g]	all-purpose flour
1 tsp	baking soda
¾ tsp	kosher salt
1½ cups [300 g]	light brown sugar, packed
1	large egg, at room temperature
1	large egg yolk, at room temperature
1 tsp	vanilla extract
1 cup [170 g]	white chocolate chips
1 cup [120 g]	dry roasted salted macadamia nuts, finely chopped

Macadamia nut cookies are my dad's favorite. Without fail, whenever we went to the mall together, he'd promptly disappear as soon as we arrived and come back with a white chocolate macadamia nut cookie in hand (and a chocolate chip cookie for me) from Mrs. Fields. So, in his honor, I've decided to take it upon myself to perfect this cookie. My version includes a brown sugar cookie base to complement the rich, salted, roasted macadamias; white chocolate chips to bring in some sweetness; and brown butter to add depth. Dare I say these cookies rival a classic chocolate chip cookie? For extra caramel notes, I suggest swapping the white chocolate for chopped caramelized white chocolate (see page 18) or Valrhona Dulcey.

DIRECTIONS

1   Place the butter into an even layer in a light-colored, wide-bottom skillet and heat over medium heat. While stirring constantly, melt the butter and cook until the milk solids turn dark brown and you smell a nutty aroma, 5 to 7 minutes. Immediately pour into a heatproof bowl to stop the cooking.

2   Let the butter cool until it reaches a solidified, room-temperature state. To speed up this process, put the bowl in the freezer for about 30 minutes, scraping down the sides of the bowl every 10 minutes.

3   In a medium bowl, combine the flour, baking soda, and salt and set aside.

4   In the bowl of a stand mixer fitted with the paddle attachment, beat the butter and sugar on medium speed for 5 minutes, until light and fluffy and pale in color. Add the egg and egg yolk one at a time until each is incorporated. Add the vanilla and beat on medium speed until fully combined. Scrape down the paddle and bowl. $\longrightarrow$

5   Add the flour mixture and beat on low speed just until combined, about 30 seconds. Add the white chocolate chips and chopped macadamia nuts and mix on low speed to incorporate, 5 to 10 seconds. Cover the bowl with plastic wrap and refrigerate for 1 hour to let all the ingredients get to know each other.

6   Adjust the oven rack to the middle position and preheat the oven to 350°F [175°C]. Line a baking sheet with parchment paper.

7   Scoop the cookies using a 1 oz cookie scoop and arrange on the prepared baking sheet spaced 2 in [5 cm] apart. Bake for 10 to 12 minutes. Transfer the baking sheet to a wire rack and let the cookies cool completely before removing from the sheet. Store the cookies in an airtight container at room temperature for up to 3 days.

TO FREEZE THE COOKIE DOUGH

Place the parchment paper–lined baking sheet with the scooped dough in the freezer for about 20 minutes, until the dough balls are set, then transfer the cookie dough to a plastic bag or freezer-safe container and stash in the freezer for up to 1 month.

VARIATION

Maple Pecan Cookies: Substitute the brown sugar with 1¼ cups [250 g] light brown sugar and ¼ cup [80 g] real maple syrup. Add ¾ tsp maple extract along with the vanilla in step 4. Substitute an equal amount of chopped toasted pecans for the macadamia nuts.

PEANUT BUTTER MILK CHOCOLATE SHORTBREAD

MAKES 24 COOKIES	
5 Tbsp [71 g]	unsalted butter, at room temperature
4 Tbsp [65 g]	creamy peanut butter
½ cup [100 g]	light brown sugar, packed
1	egg yolk
½ tsp	vanilla extract
1 cup [125 g]	all-purpose flour, plus more for dusting
¼ tsp	kosher salt
3 oz [85 g]	milk chocolate, chopped
¼ cup [35 g]	salted roasted peanuts, finely chopped
1	egg, beaten
Demerara or turbinado sugar, for rolling	

To me, shortbread tastes like Christmas and makes the perfect gift for loved ones during the holiday season. Here, the timeless, buttery elegance of classic shortbread meets the creamy allure of peanut butter, resulting in a cookie that is ultra-buttery, perfectly salty, and delightfully nutty, with a crisp yet tender bite. Perfect with a warm cup of tea or hot cocoa, this treat pays homage to simple ingredients and encapsulates the warmth of the holiday season. For best results, rest the shortbread dough overnight, as it intensifies the flavor and results in a more complex and delicious cookie.

DIRECTIONS

1   In the bowl of a stand mixer fitted with the paddle attachment, beat the butter, peanut butter, and sugar on medium speed until light and fluffy. Scrape down the bowl, then add the egg yolk and vanilla and beat for another minute until well combined. Add the flour and salt and mix on low speed just until incorporated. Scrape down the bowl again, add the chopped chocolate and peanuts, and mix just until combined.

2   Transfer the dough onto a piece of plastic wrap and, using floured hands, form into a 12 in [30 cm] log about 2 in [5 cm] in diameter. Tightly wrap the log and seal the ends by twisting the plastic wrap like a candy wrapper. Chill in the refrigerator for at least 4 hours or ideally overnight. Do not skip this step, as the cookie dough needs to be sufficiently chilled in order to slice it.   →

3   Preheat the oven to 350°F [175°C]. Line a
baking sheet with parchment paper. Unwrap
the dough and brush the exterior of the log
with the beaten egg, then carefully roll in the
demerara sugar, gently pressing the sugar into
the log. Slice the log into ½ in [13 mm] thick
rounds using a sharp knife. Arrange the cookies
on the prepared baking sheet spaced about 2 in
[5 cm] apart.

4   Bake for 12 to 15 minutes, or until the cookie
edges are golden brown. Transfer the baking
sheet to a wire rack and let cool completely.
Store the cookies in an airtight container at
room temperature for up to 5 days.

TO FREEZE THE COOKIE DOUGH

The cookie dough can be stored, tightly
wrapped in plastic and aluminum foil, in
the freezer for up to 1 month.

TRIPLE CHOCOLATE COOKIES

MAKES 24 COOKIES	
2 cups [250 g]	all-purpose flour
¾ cup [64 g]	Dutch-process cocoa powder
1 tsp	baking soda
1 tsp	kosher salt
8 oz [225 g]	caramelized white chocolate, homemade (page 18) or store-bought (such as Valrhona Dulcey fèves), divided
5 oz [140 g]	milk chocolate, roughly chopped
1 cup [225 g]	unsalted butter, at room temperature
1 cup [200 g]	dark brown sugar, packed
½ cup [100 g]	granulated sugar
1	large egg, at room temperature
1	large egg yolk, at room temperature
1 tsp	vanilla extract
Flaky sea salt, for sprinkling	

Sometimes more is more when it comes to chocolate, as is the case with these decadent Triple Chocolate Cookies, which are a veritable chocolate bomb in cookie form. The creamy notes from the caramelized white chocolate and milk chocolate perfectly complement the bitter notes of the cocoa powder. If that wasn't enough, the cookies are topped with a big chunk of chocolate to create the most inviting, melty pools of chocolate—a must for looks and taste.

DIRECTIONS

1   In a medium bowl, combine the flour, cocoa powder, baking soda, and salt and set aside.

2   Roughly chop 5 oz [140 g] of the caramelized white chocolate. Combine with the milk chocolate and set aside. Chop the remaining 3 oz [85 g] of caramelized white chocolate into ½ in [13 mm] pieces to use for topping and set aside. (Alternatively, you can top the cookies with 3 oz [85 g] milk chocolate if preferred.)

3   In the bowl of a stand mixer fitted with the paddle attachment, beat the butter and both sugars on medium speed for 5 minutes, until light and fluffy and pale in color. Add the egg and egg yolk one at a time until each is incorporated. Add the vanilla and beat for another minute, until fully combined. Scrape down the paddle and bowl, then add the flour mixture and beat on low speed just until combined, about 30 seconds. Scrape down the bowl, add the combined chopped white and milk chocolate, and mix on low speed to incorporate, 5 to 10 seconds.   →

4   Line a baking sheet with parchment paper. Using a 1 oz cookie scoop, portion the cookie dough and place on the baking sheet. Cover tightly with plastic wrap and refrigerate for at least 24 hours or up to 72 hours.

5   Adjust the oven rack to the middle position and preheat the oven to 350°F [175 °C]. Line two baking sheets with parchment paper and arrange the cookies, spacing them 2 in [5 cm] apart. Top each cookie ball with a fève or a ½ in [13 mm] piece of caramelized white chocolate or milk chocolate to create those gooey, melty pools of chocolate.

6   Bake for 10 to 12 minutes. As soon as the cookies come out of the oven, sprinkle them with flaky sea salt. Transfer the baking sheet to a wire rack and let the cookies cool completely before removing from the sheet. Store the cookies in an airtight container at room temperature for up to 3 days.

TO FREEZE THE COOKIE DOUGH

Place the parchment paper–lined baking sheet with the scooped dough in the freezer for about 20 minutes, until the dough balls are set, then transfer the cookie dough to a plastic bag or freezer-safe container and stash for up to 1 month.

COCOA-TAHINI MARBLE COOKIES

MAKES 18 COOKIES	
1½ cups [190 g]	all-purpose flour
½ tsp	baking powder
½ tsp	baking soda
½ tsp	kosher salt
½ cup [115 g]	unsalted butter, at room temperature
½ cup [130 g]	tahini
¾ cup [150 g]	dark brown sugar, packed
¼ cup [50 g]	granulated sugar
1	egg, at room temperature
1	egg yolk, at room temperature
1 tsp	vanilla extract
¼ cup [20 g]	Dutch-process cocoa powder

There's something so mesmerizing about marble cookies—not only are they eye-catching, but they also deliver a delicious contrast of flavors. These not-too-sweet cookies are the perfect combination of rich chocolate and nutty tahini. They have a delicate, tender texture like a soft sugar cookie with just the right amount of chewiness. To achieve the perfect marble effect, I like to pinch off a small amount of cookie dough and press it directly into a cookie scoop, alternating between the two flavors like a checkerboard pattern. Although it may take a bit more time, using a cookie scoop ensures consistent results so each cookie is roughly the same size.

DIRECTIONS

1 In a medium bowl, whisk together the flour, baking powder, baking soda, and salt and set aside.

2 In the bowl of a stand mixer fitted with the paddle attachment, beat the butter and tahini on medium speed until combined. Add both sugars and beat until light and fluffy, 2 to 3 minutes. With the mixer running on low speed, add the egg and egg yolk one at a time, then add the vanilla. Scrape down the bowl and add the flour mixture, mixing just until incorporated and no streaks remain.

3 Divide the dough in half, leaving one portion in the mixer and putting the other in a medium bowl. Add the cocoa powder to the dough in the mixer and beat on low speed just until combined, scraping down the bowl as needed. Cover the bowls with plastic wrap and chill for at least 1 to 2 hours since the dough is quite soft.

4 Preheat the oven to 350°F [175°C]. Line a baking sheet with parchment paper. →

5   To create the marble swirl, using a 1 oz cookie scoop, pinch a small portion of the cookie dough and press it directly into the cookie scoop, alternating between the two doughs in a loose checkerboard fashion. Once the scoop is full, compact the dough into the scoop using the heel of your palm. Alternatively, you can pinch off roughly 1 Tbsp of each dough and roll them together into a ball between the palms of your hands.

6   Arrange the cookie dough balls on the prepared baking sheet, spaced 2 in [5 cm] apart. Bake for 9 to 11 minutes. Transfer the baking sheet to a wire rack and let the cookies cool completely on the sheet. Store the cookies in an airtight container at room temperature for up to 3 days.

TO FREEZE THE COOKIE DOUGH

Place the parchment paper–lined baking sheet with the scooped dough in the freezer for about 20 minutes, until the dough balls are set, then transfer the cookie dough to a plastic bag or freezer-safe container and stash in the freezer for up to 1 month.

BANANA BUCKWHEAT
CHOCOLATE CHUNK COOKIES

MAKES 23 COOKIES	
¾ cup [170 g]	unsalted butter, cubed
1½ cups [190 g]	all-purpose flour
½ cup [65 g]	buckwheat flour
1 tsp	baking soda
¾ tsp	kosher salt
⅓ cup [85 g]	mashed banana, about 1 small banana
1 tsp	lemon juice
¾ cup [150 g]	light brown sugar, packed
½ cup [100 g]	granulated sugar
1	egg yolk, at room temperature
1 tsp	vanilla extract
6 oz [170 g]	semisweet or milk chocolate, roughly chopped
Flaky sea salt, for sprinkling	

NOTE ○ You can substitute the buckwheat flour with rye flour for an equally delicious cookie.

I was first introduced to alternative flours when I worked at Manresa Bread, where they freshly mill their flours and are big advocates of heritage grains. My short time spent there really opened my eyes to a world of new flavors. Buckwheat is one of my personal favorite grains to bake with. The nutty, deeply earthy flavor goes so well with the sweet and bitter notes of chocolate and toasty brown butter. For these cookies, I use a blend of all-purpose flour for texture and buckwheat for flavor, delivering the best of both worlds. And for an extra twist, a subtle hint of banana adds another layer of flavor and makes the cookies extra chewy so every bite is an unforgettable delight.

DIRECTIONS

1 In a wide skillet over medium-low heat, brown the butter, whisking constantly, 5 to 7 minutes. Once the milk solids look toasted and the butter turns a golden color, transfer to a bowl to cool slightly, scraping all the milk solids from the skillet along with the melted butter.

2 In a medium bowl, whisk together both flours, the baking soda, and salt. Set aside. In a separate small bowl, mix together the mashed banana and lemon juice to prevent the banana from browning. Set aside.

3 In a stand mixer fitted with the paddle attachment, beat the brown butter and both sugars on medium speed until well combined, about 2 minutes. Scrape down the bowl and add the egg yolk, then the vanilla. Mix on medium speed for another minute. Scrape down the bowl again. Add the mashed banana and mix until well combined. With the mixer on low speed, add the flour mixture and mix just until combined, about 30 seconds. Add the chopped chocolate and mix on low speed just until incorporated. →

4   Line a baking sheet with parchment paper. Using a 1 oz cookie scoop, portion the cookie dough and place on the baking sheet. Cover tightly with plastic wrap and refrigerate for at least 24 hours or up to 72 hours for maximum flavor and texture. It's important to give the buckwheat flour time to hydrate and soak up all the flavors, so don't skip this step!

5   Preheat the oven to 350°F [175°C] and line two baking sheets with parchment paper. Arrange the cookies on the prepared baking sheets about 2 in [5 cm] apart.

6   Bake for 10 to 12 minutes, until golden brown. As soon as they come out of the oven, sprinkle each cookie with a pinch of flaky sea salt. Don't worry if the cookies spread a little. Simply use a large biscuit cutter (larger than the size of the cookie) and swirl the cookie in a circular motion to shape it into a circle. Transfer the baking sheet to a wire rack and let the cookies cool completely on the sheet. Store the cookies in an airtight container at room temperature for up to 3 days.

TO FREEZE THE COOKIE DOUGH

Place the parchment paper–lined baking sheet with the scooped dough in the freezer for about 20 minutes, until the dough balls are set, then transfer the cookie dough to a plastic bag or freezer-safe container and stash in the freezer for up to 1 month.

VERY BEST CHOCOLATE CHUNK COOKIES

MAKES 36 COOKIES	
3 cups [375 g]	all-purpose flour (see Note)
1¼ tsp	kosher salt
1 tsp	baking soda
1 cup [225 g]	unsalted butter, at room temperature
1¼ cups [250 g]	light brown sugar, packed
½ cup [100 g]	granulated sugar
1	egg, at room temperature
1	large egg yolk, at room temperature
2 tsp	vanilla bean paste or extract
8 oz [225 g]	dark or semisweet chocolate, roughly chopped
Flaky sea salt, for sprinkling	

NOTE ○ For a chewier texture, use a combination of 2 cups [250 g] all-purpose flour and 1 cup [125 g] bread flour. (The higher protein content in the bread flour results in more chew.)

Chocolate chip cookies are the epitome of perfection; there's nothing better than a warm, gooey chocolate chip cookie fresh out of the oven. This recipe checks all the boxes for me: a crisp exterior, chewy texture, slightly underbaked center, and melty pools of chocolate chunks in every bite. The egg yolk adds extra richness, and the higher ratio of brown sugar gives the cookie deep caramel notes. To maximize the flavor and texture, refrigerate the cookie dough for at least 24 hours. At the bakery I worked at, we always let the cookie dough rest for a minimum of 48 hours. Resting the dough allows the flour to hydrate and lets all the flavors meld. I know it's hard to wait, but it makes all the difference. Don't forget to use the best quality chocolate and sprinkle the cookies with flaky sea salt for the ultimate sweet-and-salty combo.

DIRECTIONS

1 In a medium bowl, whisk together the flour, salt, and baking soda. Set aside.

2 In a stand mixer fitted with the paddle attachment, cream the butter and both sugars on medium speed until light and fluffy, about 5 minutes. Scrape down the paddle and bowl, then add the egg, egg yolk, and vanilla and mix on medium speed for another minute. Scrape down the paddle and bowl again. With the mixer on low speed, add the flour mixture and mix just until combined, about 30 seconds. Add the chopped chocolate and mix on low speed just until incorporated.

3 Line a baking sheet with parchment paper. Using a 1 oz cookie scoop, portion the cookie dough and place on the baking sheet. Cover tightly with plastic wrap and refrigerate for at least 24 hours or up to 72 hours. →

4   Preheat the oven to 350°F [175°C] and line two baking sheets with parchment paper. Arrange the cookies on the prepared baking sheets, spaced 2 in [5 cm] apart.

5   Bake for 10 to 12 minutes, until golden brown. As soon as the cookies come out of the oven, sprinkle them with flaky sea salt. Let the cookies cool completely on the baking sheet and store in an airtight container for up to 3 days.

TO FREEZE THE COOKIE DOUGH

Place the parchment paper–lined baking sheet with the scooped dough in the freezer for about 20 minutes, until the dough balls are set, then transfer the cookie dough to a plastic bag or freezer-safe container and stash in the freezer for up to 1 month.

VARIATIONS

Brown Butter Chocolate Chunk Cookies: Increase the butter to 1 cup plus 3 Tbsp [268 g] unsalted butter (to account for water loss while cooking) and brown the butter in a skillet following the method in steps 1 and 2 on page 47.

Miso Toffee Chocolate Chunk Cookies: Add 3½ Tbsp white miso to the butter-sugar mixture in step 2. Fold in 1 cup [160 g] toffee bits with the chopped chocolate.

ESPRESSO CHOCOLATE RYE SABLÉS

MAKES 30 COOKIES	
4 oz [115 g]	60% to 70% dark chocolate
¾ cup [95 g]	all-purpose flour
½ cup [55 g]	dark rye flour
¼ cup [20 g]	Dutch-process cocoa powder or black cocoa powder
1½ tsp	espresso powder
½ tsp	baking soda
½ tsp	kosher salt
9 Tbsp [127 g]	unsalted butter, at room temperature
½ cup [100 g]	dark brown sugar, packed
¼ cup [50 g]	granulated sugar
1	egg yolk, at room temperature
1 tsp	vanilla extract
4 oz [115 g]	white chocolate or caramelized white chocolate, homemade (page 18) or store-bought, chopped

These chocolate sablés are my definition of the ideal cookie. I learned this recipe in pastry school, and it has been a personal favorite ever since. I've adapted it ever so slightly by adding rye flour for more depth, an egg yolk for extra richness, and espresso powder to enhance the chocolate flavor even more. What makes this recipe a cut above the rest is the grated chocolate. Albeit a bit of a workout, the grated chocolate is 100 percent worth the extra effort. It is folded into the dough and melts into the cookie while baked, which results in an assertive, complex chocolate flavor.

DIRECTIONS

1   Finely grate the dark chocolate using a Microplane. If you get tired, you can use a small food processor to grind the chocolate into fine bits. Get it as close as possible to a powder consistency, pulsing for just a few seconds at a time. Set aside.

2   In a medium bowl, sift together both flours, the cocoa powder, espresso powder, baking soda, and salt and set aside.

3   In the bowl of a stand mixer fitted with the paddle attachment, beat together the butter and both sugars on medium speed until light and fluffy, 3 to 4 minutes. Scrape down the bowl and add the egg yolk and vanilla, beating until combined.

4   Add the flour mixture and mix on low speed until incorporated. Scrape down the bowl again and add the grated chocolate, mixing just until combined. Add the white chocolate and briefly mix until distributed. The dough will be crumbly, like pie dough.   →

5   Scrape the dough onto a work surface and gently form it into a ball. Roll the dough out to a ¼ in [6 mm] thickness in between two large pieces of parchment paper. Transfer the dough to a baking sheet and refrigerate for about 1 hour, until firm. Alternatively, you can roll the dough into a log like in the Peanut Butter Milk Chocolate Shortbread (page 51).

6   Preheat the oven to 325°F [160°C]. Line a baking sheet with parchment paper.

7   Cut the dough into 1¼ in [3 cm] squares using a ruler and pizza cutter or sharp knife, or into circles using a cookie cutter. (If you rolled your dough into a log, cut the log into rounds ¼ in [6 mm] thick.) Transfer the cookies to the prepared baking sheet, leaving ½ in [13 mm] of space between each cookie.

8   Bake for 12 to 14 minutes, then let cool on the baking sheet for 10 minutes before transferring to a wire rack. Store the cookies in an airtight container at room temperature for up to 3 days.

BROWNIES AND BARS

Nº 3

CHOCOLATE LOVER

WHITE CHOCOLATE CHAI DOODLES

MAKES 24 BARS	
CHAI SUGAR	
⅓ cup [67 g]	granulated sugar
1 tsp	ground cinnamon
1 tsp	ground cardamom
½ tsp	ground ginger
¼ tsp	ground allspice
¼ tsp	ground cloves
CHAI SNICKERDOODLES	
2½ cups [315 g]	all-purpose flour
1 tsp	cream of tartar
½ tsp	baking soda
½ tsp	kosher salt
1 cup [225 g]	unsalted butter, at room temperature
1 cup [200 g]	granulated sugar
½ cup [100 g]	light brown sugar, packed
2	eggs, at room temperature
2 tsp	vanilla extract
1 cup [170 g]	white chocolate chips

As the leaves start to turn and the air gets crisper, there's nothing quite like the comforting warmth of chai spices to get you in the mood for fall. The aromatic blend of cinnamon, cardamom, ginger, allspice, and cloves combined with the creamy white chocolate make these cookie bars taste like a cozy, warm hug in every bite—truly a flavor combination that can't be beat. Just like traditional snickerdoodle cookies, the cream of tartar gives these doodle bars their signature tang. These cookie bars have a soft, chewy texture with a slightly crisp exterior from the chai-spiced sugar on top.

DIRECTIONS

1 **For the Chai Sugar:** In a small bowl, whisk together the sugar and spices. Set aside.

2 **For the Chai Snickerdoodles:** Preheat the oven to 350°F [175°C]. Grease and line a 9 by 13 in [23 by 33 cm] baking pan with parchment paper, leaving an overhang on two sides.

3 In a medium bowl, whisk together the flour, cream of tartar, baking soda, and salt. Set aside. →

4   In the bowl of a stand mixer fitted with the paddle attachment or in a large bowl with a hand mixer, cream the butter and both sugars together on medium speed until light and fluffy, 2 to 3 minutes. Scrape down the bowl, then beat in the eggs one at a time, followed by the vanilla, mixing until well combined, 1 minute more. Scrape down the bowl again, then add in the flour mixture, mixing on low speed just until combined. Fold in the white chocolate chips.

5   Spread the cookie dough into the prepared pan, using an offset spatula to smooth it out into an even layer. Sprinkle the top with the chai sugar.

6   Bake for 20 to 25 minutes, or until a tooth-pick inserted into the center comes out clean. Transfer to a wire rack and let cool completely in the pan. Using the parchment sling, gently lift the bars out of the pan and cut into 24 pieces. Store the doodles in an airtight container at room temperature for up to 3 days.

VARIATIONS

Pumpkin Chai Doodles: Substitute the 2 eggs for 1 egg yolk. Add ½ cup [120 g] pumpkin purée (patted dry) after you've added the egg yolk and vanilla in step 4, before the flour mixture is added in.

Ginger Molasses Doodles: Add ½ tsp ground ginger and ½ tsp ground cinnamon to the flour mixture in step 3. Add ¼ cup [85 g] unsulfured molasses before adding the eggs in step 4 and mix until combined.

RASPBERRY SWIRL GOAT CHEESE CHEESECAKE BARS

MAKES 16 BARS	
RASPBERRY JAM	
1 tsp	cornstarch
6 oz [170 g]	fresh raspberries
2 Tbsp	granulated sugar
GRAHAM CRACKER CRUST	
1½ cups [160 g]	graham cracker crumbs (about 11 crackers)
6 Tbsp [85 g]	unsalted butter, melted
¼ cup [50 g]	granulated sugar
¼ tsp	kosher salt
FILLING	
4 oz [115 g]	white chocolate, finely chopped
1 Tbsp	lemon zest
½ cup [100 g]	granulated sugar
12 oz [340 g]	cream cheese, at room temperature
4 oz [115 g]	goat cheese, at room temperature
1 tsp	vanilla extract
½ tsp	kosher salt
½ cup [120 g]	sour cream, at room temperature
2	large eggs, at room temperature

NOTE ○ About 1 hour prior to baking, let the cream cheese, goat cheese, sour cream, and eggs come to room temperature.

These goat cheese cheesecake bars with a raspberry jam swirl are the perfect combination of tangy and sweet. The goat cheese adds a touch of sophistication and a unique twist to the classic dessert. The raspberry jam swirl not only looks beautiful but also adds a burst of tart, fruity goodness to each bite that balances the richness of the cheesecake. Homemade jam makes these extra-special, but if you don't feel up to making jam from scratch, feel free to use store-bought. Or, choose your own adventure and switch up the jam with any flavor you like.

DIRECTIONS

1 **For the Raspberry Jam:** In a small bowl, mix the cornstarch with 2 tsp of water until combined to make a slurry.

2 In a small saucepan, combine the raspberries and sugar and bring to a simmer over medium heat. Add the cornstarch slurry and cook for another 2 to 3 minutes, until thickened. Remove from the heat. To remove the seeds, strain through a fine-mesh sieve into a medium bowl. Let cool completely. →

3 **For the Graham Cracker Crust:** Preheat the oven to 350°F [175°C]. Line the bottom and sides of a 9 in [23 cm] square baking pan with parchment paper, leaving an overhang on two sides.

4 In a medium bowl, stir together the graham cracker crumbs, butter, sugar, and salt. Transfer the mixture to the prepared baking pan and pack it tightly into the bottom of the pan. Bake for 8 to 10 minutes, until the crust is toasted and fragrant. Remove from the oven and transfer to a wire rack to cool completely.

5 **For the Filling:** Melt the chopped white chocolate over a double boiler or in the microwave (see page 14).

6 In a small bowl, rub the lemon zest into the sugar to release the oils from the zest. Set aside.

7 In the bowl of a food processor, blend together the cream cheese, goat cheese, vanilla, and salt on medium speed until smooth and creamy, about 30 seconds. Scrape down the bowl, then add the lemon sugar and pulse again, until combined. Add the sour cream and pulse until smooth. Scrape down the bowl and add the eggs one at a time. Scrape down the bowl again and add the melted white chocolate, pulsing until well combined.

8 Pour the cheesecake mixture over the cooled crust and spread into an even layer using an offset spatula. Using a spoon, dot the jam over the top of the cheesecake and use a toothpick or butter knife to gently swirl the jam, making decorative swoops and swirls. Bang the pan on the counter to remove any air bubbles.

9 Bake for 20 minutes, then turn off the oven without opening the door (no peeking!) and let the cheesecake sit in the oven for 1 hour. Remove from the oven and let cool completely on a wire rack, about 1 hour. Cover and transfer to the refrigerator to set for at least 4 hours or overnight.

10 Once the cheesecake is set, run a sharp knife around the edges and carefully lift it out of the pan using the parchment sling. Cut into bars using a sharp knife, wiping the blade and dipping it into hot water between slices to get clean cuts. Cover and store in an airtight container in the fridge for up to 3 days.

VARIATION

Oreo Crust: If you prefer an Oreo cookie crust instead of the graham cracker crust, follow the cookie crust recipe from the Creamy Chocolate Cheesecake Bars on page 93.

MISO PEANUT BUTTER BLONDIES

MAKES 16 BLONDIES	
1¼ cups [156 g]	all-purpose flour
½ tsp	baking powder
¼ tsp	baking soda
¼ tsp	kosher salt
½ cup [115 g]	unsalted butter, cubed
1 cup [200 g]	dark brown sugar, packed
¼ cup [50 g]	granulated sugar
¼ cup [65 g]	creamy peanut butter
3 Tbsp	white miso
1	egg, at room temperature
1	egg yolk, at room temperature
1 tsp	vanilla extract
6 oz [170 g]	semisweet chocolate, coarsely chopped
Flaky sea salt, for sprinkling	

If you're a peanut butter lover, these cookie bars are dangerous territory. They're sweet, salty, and downright addictive. I created this recipe for my brother, who is an absolute peanut butter fanatic. When we were younger, I used to make peanut butter cookies as a bribe so he'd let me hang out with the older kids. It worked like a charm every time, and now I've reworked those magic cookies into these bars, which use miso as a secret ingredient. The umami notes of the miso perfectly complement the nutty flavors of the peanut butter, making these blondies the ideal combination of sweet and savory. And let's not forget the chunks of rich, melty chocolate that bring the indulgence factor through the roof.

DIRECTIONS

1 Preheat the oven to 350°F [175°C]. Grease and line an 8 in [20 cm] square baking pan with parchment paper, leaving an overhang on two sides.

2 In a medium bowl, whisk together the flour, baking powder, baking soda, and salt. Set aside.

3 In a wide skillet over medium-low heat, brown the butter, whisking constantly, 5 to 7 minutes. Once the milk solids look toasted and the butter turns a golden color, transfer to a large mixing bowl, scraping all the milk solids from the skillet along with the melted butter. →

4   Add both sugars to the brown butter and combine using an electric hand mixer on low speed (if you don't have an electric hand mixer, you can use a whisk). Let the mixture cool slightly, about 10 minutes. Add in the peanut butter and miso and beat on medium speed until light and fluffy. Add the egg and egg yolk one at a time, then add the vanilla. Add the flour mixture, mixing on low speed until incorporated. Fold in the chopped chocolate using a rubber spatula. Spread the blondie dough into the prepared pan and smooth the top with an offset spatula.

5   Bake for 25 to 30 minutes or until a toothpick inserted in the center comes out with moist crumbs; do not overbake. Transfer to a wire rack and let cool completely in the pan. Using the parchment sling, gently remove the blondies from the pan and cut into 16 squares using a sharp knife. Sprinkle the top with flaky sea salt before serving. Store the blondies in an airtight container at room temperature for up to 3 days.

SALTY, MALTY BLONDIES

MAKES 16 BLONDIES	
¾ cup [95 g]	all-purpose flour
¼ cup [32 g]	bread flour (see Note)
3 Tbsp	malted milk powder
¼ tsp	baking soda
½ tsp	kosher salt
10 Tbsp [140 g]	unsalted butter, cubed
1 cup [200 g]	dark brown sugar, packed
1	egg, at room temperature
1	egg yolk, at room temperature
1 tsp	vanilla extract
4 oz [115 g]	60% dark chocolate, coarsely chopped
2 oz [55 g]	semisweet chocolate, coarsely chopped
Flaky sea salt, for sprinkling	

NOTE ○ If you don't have bread flour, then sub all-purpose flour for the bread flour, using a total of 1 cup [125 g] all-purpose flour.

Chocolate chunk blondies are one of my go-to treats. They're incredibly easy to make whenever I'm craving chocolate chip cookies but I don't want a huge batch. What sets these blondies apart is the addition of malt powder, which gives them a subtle caramelized flavor and a hint of nostalgia. In addition, the mix of all-purpose flour and bread flour along with the extra egg yolk delivers a delightful chewy texture, perfect for sinking your teeth into. And, to top it off, the combination of dark and semisweet chocolate chunks makes for a more complex chocolate flavor. Feel free to include a handful of other add-ins like chopped nuts, toffee bits, or crushed pretzels to make them your own.

DIRECTIONS

1   Preheat the oven to 350°F [175°C]. Grease and line an 8 in [20 cm] square baking pan with parchment paper, leaving an overhang on two sides.

2   In a medium bowl, whisk together both flours, the malted milk powder, baking soda, and salt. Set aside.

3   In a wide skillet over medium-low heat, brown the butter, whisking constantly, 5 to 7 minutes. Once the milk solids look toasted and the butter turns a golden color, transfer to a large mixing bowl, scraping all the milk solids from the skillet along with the melted butter.   →

4   Add the sugar to the brown butter and whisk to combine. Let the mixture cool slightly, about 10 minutes. Whisk in the egg and egg yolk one at a time, then add the vanilla. Switch to a rubber spatula and fold in the flour mixture just until combined. Fold in both chopped chocolates and mix until incorporated. Spread the blondie dough into the prepared pan and smooth the top with an offset spatula.

5   Bake for 25 to 30 minutes or until a toothpick inserted in the center comes out with moist crumbs; do not overbake. Sprinkle immediately with flaky sea salt. Transfer to a wire rack and let cool completely in the pan. Using the parchment sling, gently remove the blondies from the pan and cut into 16 squares using a sharp knife. Store the blondies in an airtight container at room temperature for up to 3 days.

S'mores Blondies: Omit the malted milk powder and combine ¾ cup [90 g] finely ground graham cracker crumbs (about 6 graham crackers) with the flour mixture in step 2. Decrease the brown sugar to ¾ cup [150 g] and substitute the dark chocolate with milk or semisweet chocolate. To assemble, spread half of the blondie dough into the bottom of the baking pan and top with 1 cup [105 g] of marshmallow crème, spreading into an even layer to the edges of the pan using an offset spatula. Top with the remaining blondie dough, covering the marshmallow layer as best as possible.

ULTIMATE MILLIONAIRE PRETZEL BARS

MAKES 16 BARS	
PRETZEL SHORTBREAD	
1 cup [125 g]	all-purpose flour
½ cup [40 g]	crushed salted pretzels (from about 1 cup whole mini pretzel twists)
¼ tsp	kosher salt
½ cup [115 g]	unsalted butter, at room temperature
½ cup [100 g]	granulated sugar
1	large egg yolk
1 tsp	vanilla extract
MISO CARAMEL	
½ cup [120 g]	heavy cream
½ cup [115 g]	unsalted butter, cubed
1 cup [200 g]	granulated sugar
1 Tbsp	light corn syrup or honey
1½ Tbsp	white miso
1 tsp	vanilla extract
CHOCOLATE GANACHE	
4 oz [115 g]	semisweet or milk chocolate, chopped
¼ cup [57 g]	unsalted butter, cubed, at room temperature

These millionaire bars are essentially an elevated version of your favorite candy bar—combining sweet, salty, and umami flavors in one irresistible treat. The buttery pretzel shortbread crust provides a satisfying crunch and a touch of saltiness, while the miso caramel filling adds depth with its sweet and savory notes. And as if that wasn't enough, a decadent layer of chocolate ganache on top ties everything together in a luxurious finish.

DIRECTIONS

1 **For the Pretzel Shortbread:** Line an 8 in [20 cm] square baking pan with parchment paper, leaving an overhang on two sides.

2 In a medium bowl, mix together the flour, pretzel pieces, and salt and set aside.

3 In the bowl of a stand mixer fitted with the paddle attachment, beat the butter and sugar on medium speed until light and fluffy, about 2 minutes. Scrape down the bowl, add the egg yolk and vanilla, and mix until combined. Add the flour mixture and mix on low speed just until incorporated. Do not overbeat or you'll get a tough crust. →

4   Press the dough into the prepared pan in an even layer using your fingers. Transfer the pan to the refrigerator and chill for about 15 minutes. In the meantime, preheat the oven to 350°F [175°C]. Bake for 18 to 20 minutes, until lightly golden brown. Remove from the oven and let cool completely in the pan on a wire rack.

5   **For the Miso Caramel:** In a small saucepan over medium-low heat, gently heat the cream and butter until the butter is melted; set aside.

6   In a clean medium saucepan, add the sugar, corn syrup, and ¼ cup [60 g] of water. Using your index finger, gently incorporate the water into the sugar until the mixture resembles wet sand. Wet your hand and clean the sides of the saucepan to remove any remaining dry bits of sugar.

7   Heat the sugar over medium heat until it turns a deep amber color, 10 to 15 minutes. Resist the urge to stir, as stirring will agitate the sugar crystals and cause the sugar to seize up. Once the caramel reaches an amber color, immediately remove from the heat and carefully add the reserved cream-butter mixture. Be careful of the steam as the caramel rapidly bubbles up and sputters.

8   Return the saucepan to medium heat and cook, whisking constantly, until the caramel reaches 245°F [118°C]. Remove from the heat and whisk in the miso and vanilla, stirring until smooth and the miso is dissolved.

9   Pour the caramel over the pretzel shortbread and let cool completely in the pan.

10   **For the Chocolate Ganache:** In a small, microwave-safe bowl, add the chopped chocolate and butter. Heat in 30-second bursts until fully melted, stirring occasionally. Pour the chocolate over the cooled caramel and spread it into an even layer with an offset spatula. Allow the chocolate to set at room temperature.

11   Using the parchment sling, gently remove the shortbread from the pan and cut into sixteen 2 in [5 cm] squares using a sharp knife, wiping the blade clean and dipping it into hot water in between slices to get clean cuts. Store the bars in an airtight container at room temperature for up to 3 days.

FUDGY SHINY-TOP BROWNIES

MAKES 16 BROWNIES	
½ cup [65 g]	all-purpose flour
½ tsp	kosher salt
½ cup [115 g]	unsalted butter, cubed
4 oz [115 g]	dark chocolate, chopped
¼ cup [20 g]	Dutch-process cocoa powder
2 Tbsp	neutral oil
2	eggs
1	egg yolk
½ cup [100 g]	dark brown sugar, packed
½ cup [100 g]	granulated sugar
1 tsp	vanilla extract

Brownies will forever be my comfort treat. Thanks to my parents, I could always rely on the Costco-sized family pack of Ghirardelli brownie mix sitting on the pantry shelf just waiting to be baked at a moment's notice. Set on re-creating my favorite treat, I finally cracked the code after a dozen tests and perfected the recipe for my version of better-than-boxed brownies. In my opinion, a good brownie must be fudgy and it must have that iconic paper-thin shiny top. In order to achieve the elusive sheen, you must completely dissolve the sugar, and I've accomplished that through a unique technique. Instead of the typical method of whipping the eggs and sugar, as seen in recipes like my Crackly Top Brownies (page 89), I gently warm the egg-sugar mixture over a water bath. This ensures the sugar fully dissolves while maintaining that rich, fudgy texture we're after.

DIRECTIONS

1   Preheat the oven to 350°F [175°C]. Grease and line an 8 in [20 cm] square baking pan with parchment paper, leaving an overhang on two sides.

2   In a small bowl, whisk together the flour and salt. Set aside.

3   In a wide skillet over medium-low heat, brown the butter, whisking constantly, 5 to 7 minutes. Once the milk solids look toasted and the butter turns a golden color, transfer to a large mixing bowl, scraping all the milk solids from the skillet along with the melted butter. Combine with the chocolate and whisk until the chocolate is completely melted. Add the cocoa powder and oil to the chocolate, mix until combined, and set aside to cool slightly.

4   In a large heatproof bowl, whisk together the eggs, egg yolk, both sugars, and vanilla until well combined. Set the bowl over the saucepan, ensuring the bottom of the bowl does not touch the water. Gently heat the egg-sugar mixture to 115°F [46°C] or until the sugar dissolves, stirring frequently with a rubber spatula. Remove the bowl from the saucepan and stir in the slightly cooled chocolate mixture until well combined. Then add the flour and fold in until combined and no streaks remain.   →

5   Pour the batter into the prepared pan and bake for 30 to 35 minutes or until a toothpick comes out clean with a few moist crumbs. Transfer to a wire rack and let cool completely in the pan. Using the parchment sling, gently remove the brownies from the pan and cut into 16 squares using a sharp knife. Dip the knife in hot water and wipe clean in between cuts for clean slices. Store the brownies in an airtight container at room temperature for up to 3 days.

VARIATIONS

Stuffed Peanut Butter or Nutella Brownies: Line an 8 in [20 cm] square baking pan with parchment paper, leaving an overhang on two sides. Gently heat 1 cup [260 g] creamy peanut butter or 1 cup [260 g] Nutella in the microwave for 30 seconds to loosen it up. Spread the peanut butter or Nutella into the prepared pan and spread it into an even layer using an offset spatula. Freeze for 1 hour, until hardened and solidified.

Using the parchment paper sling, remove the frozen filling from the pan and let rest in the freezer while you prepare the brownies. Once you've made the brownie batter, spread half of the batter into the pan, then place the hardened square of peanut butter or Nutella on top and spread the remaining batter on top. Bake and store as instructed.

CRACKLY TOP BROWNIES

MAKES 16 BROWNIES	
1 cup [225 g]	unsalted butter, cubed
8 oz [225 g]	60% to 70% dark chocolate, chopped
⅓ cup [25 g]	Dutch-process cocoa powder
4	eggs, at room temperature
1 tsp	vanilla extract
1 cup [200 g]	granulated sugar
½ cup [100 g]	light brown sugar, packed
½ cup [65 g]	all-purpose flour
½ tsp	kosher salt
½ tsp	espresso powder (optional)

When it comes to brownies, the shiny, glossy top is highly coveted. But have you ever had a brownie with a crackly, meringue-like top? The crackly crust adds the perfect textural contrast and has a slight crisp that melts in your mouth. The best part is cutting into the brownies and watching the top crack with every stroke of the knife. These brownies are one of my most popular recipes for good reason. The secret to the crackly crust is whisking the eggs and sugar for 8 minutes to aerate the eggs and then gently folding in the melted chocolate and dry ingredients. I adopted this technique from the iconic flourless chocolate cake that has the same signature crust.

DIRECTIONS

1 Preheat the oven to 350°F [175°C]. Grease and line a 9 in [23 cm] square baking pan with parchment paper, leaving an overhang on two sides.

2 Melt the butter and chopped chocolate over a double boiler (see page 14), stirring frequently. Remove from the heat and stir in the cocoa powder. Set aside.

3 In a stand mixer fitted with the whisk attachment, whisk together the eggs and vanilla on low speed. Once the eggs start to get foamy, gradually add both sugars, then increase the speed to high and whisk for 8 to 10 minutes, until light and fluffy and pale in color.

4 Meanwhile, in a separate medium bowl, whisk together the flour, salt, and espresso powder, if using. Set aside.

5 Lower the mixer speed to the lowest setting and slowly pour in the melted chocolate mixture. Mix just until incorporated, 5 to 10 seconds; it's okay if there are streaks. Gently fold in the flour mixture with a rubber spatula, being careful not to overmix or deflate the eggs.

6 Pour the batter into the prepared pan and bake for 35 to 40 minutes. The tester should come out with moist, fudgy crumbs. Transfer to a wire rack and let cool completely in the pan. Using the parchment sling, gently remove the brownies from the pan and cut into 16 squares using a sharp knife. Dip the knife in hot water and wipe clean in between cuts for clean slices. Store the brownies in an airtight container at room temperature for up to 3 days.

CHEWY MOCHI BROWNIES

MAKES 16 BROWNIES	
¾ cup [110 g]	mochiko sweet rice flour
½ tsp	kosher salt
¼ tsp	baking powder
½ cup [115 g]	unsalted butter, cubed
6 oz [170 g]	60% dark chocolate, chopped and divided
¼ cup [20 g]	Dutch-process cocoa powder
2	eggs
1	egg yolk
½ cup [100 g]	granulated sugar
½ cup [100 g]	light brown sugar, packed
⅔ cup [160 g]	whole milk
1 tsp	vanilla extract

If you're team chewy brownies, then look no further. A delightful twist on the classic treat, these brownies are made with mochiko sweet rice flour, which produces the most irresistibly chewy texture. Deeply rich and fudgy from the melted chocolate and cocoa, the texture and flavor will have your taste buds dancing. Best of all, these brownies are naturally gluten-free, so everyone can enjoy them. It's important to note that you'll need mochiko sweet rice flour (which is made from a short-grained, glutinous rice) rather than regular rice flour to achieve the perfect mochi texture. You can find mochiko sweet rice flour at any Asian grocery store or online.

DIRECTIONS

1   Preheat the oven to 350°F [175°C]. Grease and line an 8 in [20 cm] square baking pan with parchment paper, leaving an overhang on two sides.

2   In a small bowl, whisk together the mochiko, salt, and baking powder. Set aside.

3   In a medium heatproof bowl, melt the butter and 4 oz [115 g] of the chopped chocolate over a double boiler (see page 14), stirring frequently. Remove the bowl from the saucepan, leaving the saucepan on the stovetop. Add the cocoa powder to the melted chocolate mixture, stir until combined, and set aside to cool slightly.

4   In a large heatproof bowl, whisk together the eggs, egg yolk, and both sugars until well combined. Set the bowl over the saucepan, ensuring the bottom of the bowl does not touch the water. Gently heat the egg-sugar mixture to 115°F [46°C] or until the sugar dissolves, stirring frequently. Remove the bowl from the saucepan and stir in the slightly cooled chocolate mixture until well combined.

5   Add the milk and vanilla and stir to combine. Add the mochiko mixture and whisk until well combined and no streaks remain.   →

6 Pour the batter into the prepared pan and top with the remaining 2 oz [57 g] chopped chocolate. Bake for 30 to 35 minutes or until a toothpick comes out clean with a few moist crumbs. Transfer to a wire rack and let cool completely in the pan. Using the parchment sling, gently remove the brownies from the pan and cut into 16 squares using a sharp knife. Dip the knife in hot water and wipe clean in between cuts for clean slices. Store the brownies in an airtight container at room temperature for up to 3 days.

CREAMY CHOCOLATE CHEESECAKE BARS

COOKIE CRUST	
24	Oreo cookies, whole with filling
¼ cup [57 g]	unsalted butter, melted
¼ tsp	kosher salt

CHOCOLATE CHEESECAKE	
16 oz [455 g]	cream cheese, at room temperature
¾ cup [150 g]	granulated sugar
⅓ cup [80 g]	sour cream, at room temperature
⅓ cup [80 g]	heavy cream, at room temperature
2	large eggs, at room temperature
4 oz [115 g]	60% to 70% dark chocolate, melted and cooled
2 tsp	vanilla extract
½ tsp	kosher salt

NOTE ◦ About 1 hour prior to baking, remove the cream cheese, heavy cream, sour cream, and eggs from the refrigerator and let come to room temperature.

These chocolate cheesecake bars are pure chocolate bliss. My favorite part about this recipe is that both the crust and the filling come together quickly and easily with the help of a food processor. I first learned about this technique while watching an episode of *America's Test Kitchen* years ago, and I've never looked back. The food processor guarantees there are no clumps of cream cheese and produces an ultra-smooth and creamy texture. Plus, there's no need for a fussy water bath, so you can enjoy these rich, decadent cheesecake bars without worrying about cracking.

DIRECTIONS

1 **For the Cookie Crust:** Preheat the oven to 350°F [175°C]. Grease and line the bottom and sides of a 9 in [23 cm] square baking pan with parchment paper, leaving an overhang on two sides.

2 In the bowl of a food processor, grind the Oreos (whole, with the cream filling) into fine crumbs. Transfer to a small mixing bowl and add the melted butter and salt, mixing to combine.

3 Spread the cookie crumbs into the prepared pan and press firmly into an even layer. I like to use the bottom of a shot glass or small measuring cup to pat it down. Bake for 5 minutes, then let cool completely. →

4 **For the Chocolate Cheesecake:** Clean the bowl of the food processor. In the bowl, pulse the cream cheese until smooth. Add the sugar and pulse for 30 seconds. Add the sour cream and heavy cream and pulse for another 30 seconds. Scrape down the bowl, then add the eggs one at a time. Scrape down the bowl again, then add the melted chocolate, vanilla, and salt. Blend until well combined and smooth, scraping down the bowl again as necessary.

5 Pour the batter over the cooled cookie crust. Bake for 20 minutes, then turn off the oven without opening the door (no peeking!) and let sit in the oven for 1 hour. Remove from the oven and let cool completely on a wire rack, about 1 hour. Cover and transfer to the refrigerator to let set for at least 4 hours or overnight.

6 Once set, run a sharp knife around the edges and lift the cheesecake out of the pan using the parchment sling. Cut the bars using a sharp knife, wiping the blade clean and dipping it into hot water in between slices to get clean cuts. Serve with a dollop of whipped cream, if desired. Store in the fridge for up to 3 days.

CHOCOLATE LOVER | LIGHT / FLUFFY | Nº 4

SNACKING CAKES

WHITE CHOCOLATE CHIP CONFETTI CAKE

MAKES ONE 8 IN [20 CM] CAKE	
WHITE CHOCOLATE CHIP **CONFETTI CAKE**	
1½ cups [190 g]	all-purpose flour
2 Tbsp	cornstarch
1½ tsp	baking powder
½ tsp	kosher salt
½ cup [115 g]	unsalted butter, at room temperature
1 cup [200 g]	granulated sugar
2	eggs, at room temperature
1½ tsp	vanilla bean paste or extract
¼ cup [60 g]	sour cream, at room temperature
½ cup [120 g]	whole milk or buttermilk, well shaken, at room temperature
½ cup [85 g]	white chocolate chips
¼ cup [40 g]	sprinkles
WHITE CHOCOLATE **CREAM CHEESE FROSTING**	
1½ oz [45 g]	white chocolate, finely chopped
4 oz [115 g]	cream cheese, at room temperature
¼ cup [57 g]	unsalted butter, at room temperature
1½ cups [180 g]	confectioners' sugar, sifted
½ tsp	vanilla extract
¼ tsp	kosher salt
Sprinkles, for topping	

It goes without saying that confetti cake is the quintessential birthday cake. This version is perfect for celebrating an occasion with a small group when a multilayer cake might be overkill, or for making a regular day a little bit sweeter. (To make this into a tiered cake, double the recipe and use two 9 in [23 cm] round pans.) White chocolate chips are folded into the batter in place of the traditional rainbow chips, while vibrant sprinkles add that essential pop of color and whimsy. You can use whatever color sprinkles you like to match the occasion, but make sure not to use nonpareils sprinkles, as they will bleed into the cake. Whether you're celebrating a special occasion or simply craving a playful dessert, indulge in this white chocolate confetti cake and let the party begin!

DIRECTIONS

1 **For the White Chocolate Chip Confetti Cake:** Preheat the oven to 350°F [175°C]. Grease and line an 8 in [20 cm] square baking pan with parchment paper, leaving an overhang on two sides.

2 In a medium bowl, whisk together the flour, cornstarch, baking powder, and salt. Set aside.

3 In a stand mixer fitted with the paddle attachment or in a large bowl with a hand mixer, beat together the butter and sugar until fluffy, about 2 minutes. Add the eggs and vanilla and mix until well combined. Scrape down the bowl, add the sour cream, and mix again until combined. →

4   With the mixer running on low speed, add half of the flour mixture, beating just until incorporated. Add in the milk and mix just until combined. Add the remaining half of the flour mixture, mixing just until incorporated and no streaks of flour remain. Fold in the white chocolate chips and sprinkles just until incorporated. Pour the batter into the prepared pan and smooth the top with an offset spatula.

5   Bake for 35 to 40 minutes or until a toothpick inserted into the center comes out clean. Let the cake cool in the pan for 10 minutes, then turn it out onto a wire rack to cool completely.

6   **For the White Chocolate Cream Cheese Frosting:** Place the white chocolate in a microwave-safe bowl and heat in the microwave in 30 second bursts until melted. Set aside.

7   In a stand mixer fitted with the paddle attachment, beat the cream cheese and butter on medium-low until smooth, 1 minute. Scrape down the bowl and add the confectioners' sugar, vanilla, and salt. Mix on low until combined and then increase the speed to medium and mix until light and fluffy. Add the melted white chocolate and beat until smooth, 2 to 3 minutes.

8   Spread the frosting over the cooled cake and decorate with sprinkles. Store the cake, covered, in the fridge for up to 3 days.

VARIATION

Cookies and Cream Cake: Substitute the sprinkles with 5 chopped Oreo cookies (whole, with the cream filling) and fold into the cake batter along with the white chocolate chips in step 4. Decorate with additional chopped Oreos if desired.

BROWN BUTTER CHOCOLATE BANANA BREAD

MAKES ONE 9 BY 5 IN [23 BY 13 CM] LOAF	
3 Tbsp	nonfat dry milk powder
1¼ cups [156 g]	all-purpose flour
½ cup [45 g]	Dutch-process cocoa powder
¾ tsp	baking powder
¾ tsp	baking soda
½ tsp	kosher salt
½ cup [115 g]	unsalted butter, cubed
2 Tbsp	neutral oil
2	eggs, at room temperature
½ cup [100 g]	dark brown sugar, packed
½ cup [100 g]	granulated sugar
1⅓ cups [325 g]	mashed ripe bananas
¼ cup [60 g]	buttermilk, well shaken, at room temperature
1 tsp	vanilla extract
1 cup [170 g]	mini semisweet chocolate chips, divided

In my house, I have one simple rule: When life gives you ripe bananas, you must make banana bread. It's simply a must-do. Although it's hard to beat the classic version, chocolate always makes everything better. To make this banana bread extra special, I add toasted milk powder and browned butter. The toasted milk powder, when combined with the browned butter, creates a super fortified and enriched blend that infuses the banana bread with an irresistible flavor. The nutty, aromatic browned butter pairs perfectly with the caramel undertones and natural sweetness of the bananas.

DIRECTIONS

1 Preheat the oven to 350°F [175°C]. Grease a 9 by 5 in [23 by 13 cm] loaf pan with nonstick spray and line it with parchment paper, leaving an overhang on two sides.

2 In a wide skillet over medium heat, toast the milk powder until it turns a golden brown color, stirring frequently for 5 to 7 minutes. Remove from the heat and transfer to a medium bowl and let cool slightly. To the same bowl, add the flour, cocoa powder, baking powder, baking soda, and salt and stir to combine, breaking up any clumps of toasted milk powder. Set aside.

3 In the same wide skillet, brown the butter over medium-low heat, whisking constantly for 5 to 7 minutes. Once the milk solids look toasted and the butter turns a golden color, transfer to a bowl to cool, scraping all the milk solids from the skillet along with the melted butter. Whisk in the oil and set aside to cool slightly. →

4   In the bowl of a stand mixer fitted with the paddle attachment, beat together the eggs and both sugars on medium speed until light and frothy, 3 to 5 minutes. Add the browned butter mixture and mix until emulsified. Add the mashed banana, buttermilk, and vanilla and mix on low speed just until combined. Mix in the flour mixture just until combined and no streaks of flour remain. Fold in ¾ cup [130 g] of the mini chocolate chips.

5   Pour the batter into the prepared pan and smooth the top with an offset spatula. Sprinkle the top with the remaining ¼ cup [40 g] mini chocolate chips. Bake for 60 to 70 minutes, or until a toothpick comes out clean. Transfer to a wire rack and let cool in the pan for 30 minutes, then remove from the pan and continue cooling completely. Store the banana bread, covered, at room temperature for up to 3 days.

VARIATION

Chocolate Chip Banana Bread: Replace the cocoa powder with ½ cup [65 g] all-purpose flour (bringing the total amount of flour used to 1¾ cups [220 g]).

ANYTIME CHOCOLATE SNACK CAKE

MAKES ONE 8 IN [20 CM] CAKE	
CHOCOLATE CAKE	
¼ cup [57 g]	unsalted butter, at room temperature
¾ cup [150 g]	light brown sugar, packed
¼ cup [50 g]	granulated sugar
¼ cup [55 g]	neutral oil
2	large eggs, at room temperature
1 cup [240 g]	sour cream or full-fat yogurt, at room temperature
1 tsp	vanilla extract
1 cup [125 g]	all-purpose flour
½ cup [45 g]	Dutch-process cocoa powder
2 Tbsp	cornstarch
½ tsp	baking soda
½ tsp	baking powder
½ tsp	kosher salt
CHOCOLATE BUTTERCREAM	
3 oz [85 g]	semisweet chocolate, finely chopped
½ cup [115 g]	unsalted butter, at room temperature
1½ Tbsp	heavy cream
½ tsp	vanilla extract
¼ tsp	kosher salt
1 cup [120 g]	confectioners' sugar, sifted
Sprinkles or chocolate pearls, for decoration	

There's something comforting about a simple chocolate snack cake—a humble treat that doesn't require a particular reason or special occasion and can be enjoyed anytime a chocolate craving strikes. It's the type of craving that hits when you're walking by the kitchen, catch a glimpse of the cake out of the corner of your eye, and find yourself quietly peeling back the plastic wrap, reaching for a fork, and taking an inconspicuous bite so nobody else notices any signs of tampering. We've all been there, and this is the perfect cake for that kind of stealth snacking. The buttercream has a rich, fudgy flavor from the melted chocolate, and the recipe uses one bowl, which means easy clean up.

DIRECTIONS

1 **For the Chocolate Cake:** Preheat the oven to 350°F [175°C]. Grease an 8 in [20 cm] square baking pan with nonstick spray and line with parchment paper.

2 In a large mixing bowl, using an electric hand mixer beat together the butter and both sugars on medium speed until well combined. Add the oil and mix until emulsified. Add the eggs one at a time, mixing thoroughly after each addition. Add the sour cream and vanilla and beat on medium speed until well combined and smooth. Add the flour, cocoa powder, cornstarch, baking soda, baking powder, and salt and mix on low speed until combined and no streaks remain. →

3 Pour the batter into the prepared cake pan and smooth the top with an offset spatula. Bake for 30 to 35 minutes or until a toothpick comes out clean and the center reads an internal temperature of 205°F [95°C]. Transfer to a wire rack and let cool completely in the pan.

4 **For the Chocolate Buttercream:** Melt the chocolate over a double boiler (see page 14) or in the microwave (see page 15) and set aside to cool.

5 In the bowl of a stand mixer fitted with the paddle attachment, beat the butter on medium speed until light and fluffy. Add the cream, vanilla, and salt and mix until combined. Scrape down the bowl and add the confectioners' sugar, starting on low speed and then increasing to medium once it's incorporated. Beat until light and fluffy, 2 to 3 minutes, then add the cooled melted chocolate and mix on low speed until fully incorporated.

6 Remove the cake from the pan and top with swirls of frosting using an offset spatula and scatter with sprinkles or chocolate pearls. Serve and enjoy anytime. Store the cake, covered, at room temperature for up to 3 days.

DOUBLE CHOCOLATE ZUCCHINI CAKE

MAKES ONE 8 IN [20 CM] CAKE	
CHOCOLATE ZUCCHINI CAKE	
½ cup [100 g]	light brown sugar, packed
½ cup [100 g]	granulated sugar
2	large eggs, at room temperature
⅓ cup [75 g]	unsalted butter, melted and cooled
¼ cup [55 g]	neutral oil
¼ cup [60 g]	sour cream, at room temperature
1 tsp	vanilla extract
1¼ cups [156 g]	all-purpose flour
½ cup [45 g]	Dutch-process cocoa powder
1 tsp	baking powder
¾ tsp	kosher salt
¼ tsp	baking soda
2 cups [225 g]	loosely packed grated zucchini (about 1 medium zucchini)
½ cup [85 g]	semisweet chocolate chips
CHOCOLATE CREAM CHEESE FROSTING	
¼ cup [57 g]	unsalted butter, at room temperature
4 oz [115 g]	cream cheese, at room temperature
1½ cups [180 g]	confectioners' sugar, sifted
¼ tsp	kosher salt
1½ oz [45 g]	dark chocolate, melted and cooled (about ¼ cup)
Sprinkles, for decoration	

Zucchini cake is always on repeat during the summer when I have an overabundance of zucchini. This cake has a rich chocolate flavor from the cocoa and chocolate chips. Similar to its distant cousin, carrot cake, this cake stays moist thanks to the grated zucchini. For those who may be skeptical, there's no trace of zucchini in the finished cake, and none will be the wiser if you don't tell them. Frosting is optional as it's good on its own, but if you're feeling extra indulgent, top with a chocolate cream cheese frosting for complete decadence.

DIRECTIONS

1 **For the Chocolate Zucchini Cake:** Preheat the oven to 350°F [175°C]. Grease an 8 in [20 cm] square baking pan with nonstick spray and line with parchment paper.

2 Pat the grated zucchini with a paper towel to remove any excess moisture and set aside. In a large mixing bowl, whisk together both sugars and the eggs until frothy, about 1 minute. Add the melted butter, oil, sour cream, and vanilla and mix until emulsified. Place a large sieve over the mixing bowl and sift the flour, cocoa powder, baking powder, salt, and baking soda into the bowl. Whisk until well combined and fully incorporated. Switch to a rubber spatula and fold in the grated zucchini and chocolate chips. $\rightarrow$

3 Transfer the batter to the prepared pan and smooth the top with an offset spatula. Bake for 30 to 35 minutes or until a toothpick comes out clean and the center reads an internal temperature of 205°F [95°C]. Transfer to a wire rack and let cool completely in the pan.

4 **For the Chocolate Cream Cheese Frosting:** In the bowl of a stand mixer fitted with the paddle attachment or in a large bowl with a hand mixer, beat the butter until smooth, about 30 seconds. Add the cream cheese and mix until well combined. Add the confectioners' sugar and salt and mix on low speed until incorporated. Increase the speed to medium and mix until smooth. Add the melted chocolate and mix until well combined, taking care not to overbeat. Remove the cake from the pan. Spread the frosting evenly over the top of the cake using an offset spatula and scatter with sprinkles. Serve and enjoy. Store the cake, covered, in the fridge for up to 3 days.

ORANGE AND OLIVE OIL CHOCOLATE CAKE

MAKES ONE 9 IN [23 CM] CAKE	
CHOCOLATE OLIVE OIL CAKE	
½ cup [120 g]	hot coffee
½ cup [45 g]	Dutch-process cocoa powder
1 cup [125 g]	all-purpose flour
1 tsp	baking soda
½ tsp	baking powder
½ tsp	kosher salt
1 cup [200 g]	granulated sugar
2 tsp	orange zest
2	eggs, at room temperature
½ cup [115 g]	extra-virgin olive oil
½ cup [120 g]	buttermilk, well shaken, at room temperature
½ tsp	vanilla extract
CHOCOLATE GANACHE	
4 oz [115 g]	dark chocolate, finely chopped
½ cup [120 g]	heavy cream

There's something so captivating about the fragrant aroma of fresh oranges paired with the bitter taste of extra-virgin olive oil. This simple yet elegant cake celebrates the marriage of these two ingredients, resulting in a tender and moist crumb that's infused with subtle citrus undertones. To maximize the orange flavor, I like to rub the sugar together with the orange zest to release the oils and infuse the sugar. The olive oil adds a subtle richness to the cake while also lending a slight bitterness that balances out the sweetness of the chocolate. The cake is then topped with a luscious chocolate ganache that takes it to a whole new level of decadence. For the best flavor, use high-quality olive oil.

DIRECTIONS

1 **For the Chocolate Olive Oil Cake:** Preheat the oven to 350°F [175°C]. Grease the bottom of a 9 in [23 cm] round cake pan with nonstick spray and line with parchment paper.

2 In a small bowl or large glass measuring cup, stir together the coffee and cocoa powder to combine. Set aside to allow the cocoa powder to bloom.

3 In a medium bowl, whisk together the flour, baking soda, baking powder, and salt.

4 In a large bowl, rub the sugar and orange zest together to release the oils from the zest. Add the eggs and whisk until well combined, about 1 minute. Add the olive oil and whisk until emulsified, another 30 seconds. Add the buttermilk and vanilla and beat until well combined. Add the flour mixture and mix just until combined and no streaks of flour remain. $\longrightarrow$

5   Pour the batter into the prepared pan and smooth the top with an offset spatula. Bake for 30 to 35 minutes, or until a toothpick comes out clean and the center is set. Transfer to a wire rack and let cool completely in the pan.

6   **For the Chocolate Ganache:** Place the chopped chocolate in a medium heatproof bowl. In a small saucepan over medium heat, heat the cream until it comes to a boil. Remove from the heat and pour the hot cream over the chocolate. Let sit for 1 minute, undisturbed, to soften the chocolate.

7   Using a whisk, mix until the chocolate is fully incorporated and melted. Let the ganache cool slightly. Remove the cake from the pan and pour the ganache over the top of the cake, smoothing it out with an offset spatula as needed. Store the cake, covered, at room temperature for up to 3 days.

VARIATION

Earl Grey, Orange, and Olive Oil Cake: Substitute Earl Grey tea for the coffee. I like to steep two tea bags in ¾ cup [180 g] of water to make an extra strong cup of tea. The orange zest in the cake brings out the bergamot undertones in the Earl Grey tea, making it a lovely pairing.

CHOCOLATE RICOTTA MARBLE POUND CAKE

MAKES ONE 9 BY 5 IN [23 BY 13 CM] LOAF	
3 Tbsp	Dutch-process cocoa powder, sifted
3 Tbsp	boiling water
1½ oz [45 g]	60% to 70% dark chocolate, melted (about ¼ cup)
1½ cups [190 g]	all-purpose flour
2 Tbsp	cornstarch
2½ tsp	baking powder
1 tsp	kosher salt
½ cup [115 g]	unsalted butter, at room temperature
1½ cups [360 g]	whole-milk ricotta, well drained (see Note)
¼ cup [55 g]	neutral oil
1½ cups [300 g]	granulated sugar
3	large eggs, at room temperature
2 tsp	vanilla extract
2 tsp	orange zest (optional)

NOTE ○ Make sure your ricotta is well drained. About 30 minutes before you are ready to bake, fit a mesh sieve over a bowl, place the ricotta into the sieve, and let drain. Gently press with a paper towel to remove excess moisture.

Pound cake was always a staple in my house growing up—specifically the store-bought Sara Lee pound cakes. I would smother my slice with whipped cream and macerated strawberries. It was one of my favorite treats and never disappointed. But while store-bought pound cakes are convenient, there's nothing quite like homemade. This recipe has the classic buttery flavor of a pound cake with an impossibly light and tender crumb from the ricotta. The chocolate swirls add just enough chocolatey goodness without being overwhelming. Simple yet impressive in presentation, this cake can stand alone or be dressed up with whipped cream and berries to suit any occasion.

DIRECTIONS

1   Preheat the oven to 350°F [175°C]. Grease a 9 by 5 in [23 by 13 cm] loaf pan with nonstick spray and line with parchment paper, leaving an overhang on two sides.

2   In a small bowl, whisk together the cocoa powder and boiling water until well combined. Add the melted chocolate and stir to combine. Set aside.

3   In a medium bowl, sift together the flour, cornstarch, baking powder, and salt and set aside.   →

4   In the bowl of a stand mixer fitted with the paddle attachment, beat together the butter and ricotta on medium speed until light and fluffy. Scrape down the bowl, add the oil and sugar, and beat until well combined, 1 to 2 minutes. Add the eggs one at a time, mixing thoroughly after each addition. Scrape down the bowl and add the vanilla and orange zest, if using, and mix until incorporated.

5   With the mixer on low speed, add the flour mixture and mix just until combined. Transfer half the batter into another bowl. In the stand mixer bowl, fold in the cocoa mixture and mix until fully incorporated.

6   Add the batters to the prepared pan using an ice cream scoop, alternating between the two batters to create a marble effect. Swirl with a knife and smooth the top with an offset spatula. Bake for 55 to 65 minutes or until a digital thermometer registers 205°F [95°C] when inserted into the center. Transfer to a wire rack and let cool in the pan for 30 minutes, then remove from the pan with the parchment sling and continue cooling completely. Store the cake, covered, at room temperature for up to 3 days.

CELEBRATION CAKES

HIP HIP / HOORAY

CHOCOLATE LOVER

STRAWBERRY WHITE CHOCOLATE CHANTILLY CAKE

MAKES ONE 8 IN [20 CM] THREE-LAYER CAKE	
WHITE CHOCOLATE CHANTILLY	
4 oz [115 g]	white chocolate, finely chopped
1¾ cups [420 g]	cold heavy cream, divided
8 oz [225 g]	cold cream cheese
1½ cups [180 g]	confectioners' sugar, sifted
8 oz [225 g]	cold mascarpone
½ tsp	kosher salt
ALMOND-VANILLA CAKE	
3 cups [375 g]	all-purpose flour
¼ cup [32 g]	cornstarch
4 tsp	baking powder
1 tsp	kosher salt
2 cups [400 g]	granulated sugar
½ cup [115 g]	unsalted butter, at room temperature
½ cup [115 g]	neutral oil
4	large eggs, at room temperature
½ cup [120 g]	sour cream, at room temperature
1 Tbsp	vanilla extract
½ tsp	almond extract
1 cup [240 g]	whole milk, at room temperature
1 lb [455 g]	fresh strawberries, for filling and decoration, divided

VARIATION

Strawberry Chantilly: For an extra punch of strawberry and a pop of pink color, grind 2 cups [34 g] of freeze-dried strawberries into a fine powder and add in with the heavy cream.

My family has been loyal devotees of the famous Whole Foods Chantilly cake for years. It's one of the most requested cakes in our house and has been a fixture at many celebrations. I've also been known to buy it by the slice for a quick weekday fix. Inspired by the original, I recreated it into an almond cake with white chocolate Chantilly. The original Chantilly recipe uses both mascarpone and cream cheese, though I've subbed in white chocolate for half of the sugar, which adds sweetness and results in an extra-stabilized cream with a smooth texture. Paired with strawberries scattered in between the cake layers, this cake has become my family's new favorite.

DIRECTIONS

1 **For the White Chocolate Chantilly:**
In a large mixing bowl, add the chopped white chocolate.

2 In a small saucepan over medium heat, heat ¾ cup [180 g] of the heavy cream and bring it just to a boil. Remove from the heat and pour over the chopped white chocolate. Whisk to combine until the chocolate is melted and the mixture is emulsified. Let cool slightly, then transfer to the refrigerator and let cool completely, 1 to 2 hours. →

3 In the bowl of a stand mixer fitted with the paddle attachment, beat the cream cheese and confectioners' sugar until smooth, ensuring there are no lumps. Scrape down the bowl, then add the mascarpone and mix until fully combined. Scrape down the bowl again and switch to the whisk attachment. Add the remaining 1 cup [240 g] of heavy cream, the cold chocolate mixture, and the salt. Whisk on low speed until the cream and chocolate mixture become incorporated, then increase the speed to medium and whisk until ribbons begin to form. Keep an eye on it and take care not to overwhip; the mixture should hold soft peaks. Cover and chill until ready to use.

4 **For the Almond-Vanilla Cake:** Preheat the oven to 350°F [175°C]. Grease three 8 in [20 cm] round cake pans and line the bottoms with parchment paper.

5 In a medium bowl, whisk together the flour, cornstarch, baking powder, and salt until combined.

6 In a stand mixer fitted with the paddle attachment, beat together the sugar and butter on medium speed until light and fluffy, 2 to 3 minutes. Add the oil and beat for 1 minute more, until emulsified. Scrape down the bowl. Add the eggs one at a time, incorporating completely before adding the next one. Add the sour cream, vanilla, and almond extract and mix until well combined. With the mixer running on low speed, add half of the flour mixture and beat just until combined. Pour in the milk and mix until incorporated, scraping down the bowl as needed. Add the remaining half of the flour mixture and mix just until combined and no streaks of flour remain.

7 Divide the batter evenly among the three cake pans. Bake for 30 to 35 minutes or until a toothpick inserted in the center comes out clean. Allow the cakes to cool in the pans for 10 minutes, then turn them out onto a wire rack to cool completely.

8 Set aside a few whole strawberries for decoration. Trim and chop the remaining strawberries into bite-size pieces. Trim and level the tops of the cooled cakes if needed. Freeze the cake layers for about 15 minutes to make them easier to frost.

9 Arrange the first cake layer, cut-side up, on a turntable. Spread about 1 cup [240 g] of the Chantilly evenly over the cake using an offset spatula. Scatter half of the chopped strawberries onto the cream, then top with the second layer of cake. Repeat one more time and place the third layer on top, cut-side down.

10 Crumb coat the cake by frosting the top and sides of the cake with a layer of the Chantilly cream about ¼ in [6 mm] thick. Refrigerate for 30 minutes to help set the frosting.

11 Once chilled, finish frosting the sides and top of the cake with the remaining Chantilly using an offset spatula. Use a cake scraper to clean up any gaps and create a smooth finish. Top with the remaining strawberries for decoration and transfer to a cake stand to serve. Store any leftover cake, covered, in the fridge for up to 3 days.

YELLOW CHOCOLATE CHIP BIRTHDAY CAKE

MAKES ONE 8 IN [20 CM] TWO-LAYER CAKE	
YELLOW CHOCOLATE CHIP CAKE	
2¼ cups [285 g]	unbleached cake flour, such as King Arthur
2½ tsp	baking powder
¾ tsp	kosher salt
1¾ cups [350 g]	granulated sugar
¾ cup [170 g]	unsalted butter, at room temperature
¼ cup [55 g]	neutral oil
3	large eggs, at room temperature
3	large egg yolks, at room temperature
½ cup [120 g]	sour cream, at room temperature
2 tsp	vanilla extract
½ cup [120 g]	whole milk, at room temperature
½ cup [85 g]	mini semisweet chocolate chips
WHIPPED CARAMEL CHOCOLATE GANACHE	
8 oz [225 g]	milk or dark chocolate, chopped
¼ cup [57 g]	unsalted butter, cubed, at room temperature
1½ cups [360 g]	heavy cream
1 tsp	vanilla extract
¼ tsp	kosher salt
1 cup plus 2 Tbsp [225 g]	granulated sugar

A buttery yellow cake with chocolate frosting is a timeless classic. This beloved combination is synonymous with birthdays and, for me, evokes warm memories and nostalgia. When I was a kid, the boxed yellow cake mix with the canned chocolate frosting served as my initiation into the world of baking. It was the first layer cake I ever made, and I remember presenting those double layers with such pride. Over the years, I've perfected my version of the iconic cake. I like to add mini chocolate chips to the cake batter, offering an extra hint of chocolate goodness and a little extra festivity. Adding a touch of oil to the batter keeps the cake moist, and the cake flour yields a super tender and light crumb. For a golden yellow color, be sure to use high-quality eggs that have a rich yolk color.

DIRECTIONS

1 **For the Yellow Chocolate Chip Cake:** Preheat the oven to 350°F [175°C]. Grease two 8 in [20 cm] round cake pans and line the bottoms with parchment paper.

2 In a medium bowl, whisk together the cake flour, baking powder, and salt until combined. →

3   In a stand mixer fitted with the paddle attachment, beat the sugar and butter on medium speed until light and fluffy, 2 to 3 minutes. Add the oil and beat for another minute, until emulsified. Scrape down the bowl. Add the eggs and egg yolks one at a time, incorporating completely before adding the next one. Add the sour cream and vanilla and mix until well combined. With the mixer running on low speed, add half of the flour mixture and beat just until combined. Pour in the milk and mix until incorporated, scraping down the bowl as needed. Add the remaining half of the flour mixture and mix just until combined. Fold in the mini chocolate chips with a rubber spatula and mix just until incorporated and no streaks of flour remain.

4   Divide the batter evenly among the two cake pans. Bake for 35 to 40 minutes or until a toothpick inserted in the center comes out clean. Allow the cake to cool in the pans for 15 to 20 minutes and then invert onto a wire rack to cool completely.

5   **For the Whipped Caramel Chocolate Ganache:** Add the chopped chocolate and cubed butter to a large heatproof bowl.

6   In a small saucepan over medium-low heat, bring the heavy cream, vanilla, and salt just to a boil. Remove from heat and set aside. In another saucepan, add the sugar and ¼ cup [60 g] of water. Using your index finger, gently incorporate the water into the sugar until the mixture resembles wet sand. Clean the sides of the saucepan to remove any remaining dry bits of sugar. Heat the sugar over medium heat until it turns a deep amber color, 10 to 15 minutes. Immediately remove from the heat and add the heavy cream. Be careful of the steam as the caramel bubbles up and sputters. Mix until combined and the caramel is melted. Pour over

the chopped chocolate and let sit for 5 minutes. Whisk until smooth and the chocolate is completely melted. Transfer to the refrigerator and let cool for 1 to 2 hours.

7   In the bowl of a stand mixer fitted with the whisk attachment, whip the chocolate ganache on medium speed until stiff peaks form, 30 to 60 seconds. Be careful not to overwhip, or the ganache will turn grainy.

8   **To Assemble:** Trim and level the tops of the cooled cakes if needed. Freeze the cake layers for about 15 minutes to make them easier to frost.

9   Arrange the first cake layer cut-side up on a turntable. Spread the whipped ganache on top and evenly distribute using an offset spatula. Stack the next layer of cake on top. Frost the top and sides of the cake with the remaining frosting. Use a cake scraper to clean up any gaps and create a smooth finish. Top with the mini chocolate chips or sprinkles for decoration and transfer the cake to a cake stand to serve. Store, covered, in the fridge for up to 3 days.

VARIATIONS

Ganache Flavor Variations: Infuse the heavy cream with 1 tsp of loose-leaf tea, 1 tsp of espresso powder, ¼ cup [30 g] malted milk powder, or 1 split vanilla bean to add an extra boost of flavor. Follow the instructions on page 19 to infuse the cream, then continue following the steps above.

CHOCOLATE STOUT RYE BUNDT

MAKES ONE BUNDT CAKE	
CHOCOLATE STOUT CAKE	
1½ cups [190 g]	all-purpose flour
¾ cup [80 g]	dark rye flour
2 tsp	baking soda
1 tsp	baking powder
¾ tsp	kosher salt
1 cup [240 g]	chocolate stout beer (see Note)
½ cup [115 g]	unsalted butter, cubed
1 cup [85 g]	Dutch-process cocoa powder
2	large eggs, at room temperature
1 cup [200 g]	granulated sugar, plus more for dusting
1 cup [200 g]	dark brown sugar, packed
¾ cup [180 g]	sour cream, at room temperature
½ cup [115 g]	neutral oil
2 tsp	vanilla extract
IRISH CREAM GANACHE	
4 oz [115 g]	caramelized white chocolate, homemade (page 18) or store-bought, or dark chocolate, chopped
½ cup [120 g]	heavy cream
1 Tbsp	Bailey's Irish Cream
Pinch	kosher salt

NOTE ○ If you can't find chocolate stout, substitute your favorite stout. Peanut butter stout is also highly recommended!

This cake is a year-round favorite that's not just reserved for St. Patrick's Day. Rich and decadent without being overly sweet, it benefits from the use of a high-quality stout, preferably a chocolate stout. This lends an incredible moistness to the cake and imparts a subtle bitterness that cuts through the sweetness of the chocolate, while the rye adds an unexpected depth of flavor. I like to make this a day ahead to allow the flavors to meld and the stout's intensity to mellow slightly. Of course, it's only fitting to crown this cake with a dreamy white chocolate ganache, and I recommend using Valrhona Dulcey for its butterscotch undertones. (You can also substitute the white chocolate in the ganache with dark chocolate for added richness.) The striking contrast between the chocolate cake and caramel-colored ganache creates a visual reminiscent of a frothy beer.

DIRECTIONS

1 **For the Chocolate Stout Cake:** Preheat the oven to 350°F [175°C]. Generously grease a 12-cup Bundt pan with nonstick spray or softened butter. Lightly sprinkle the bottom and sides with granulated sugar, discarding any excess. (I find that sugar creates a nice crust around the bottom edge, and the cake always releases cleanly from the pan.)

2 In a medium bowl, whisk together both flours, the baking soda, baking powder, and salt. →

3   In a large saucepan over medium heat, bring the stout and butter to a gentle simmer. Remove from the heat and whisk in the cocoa powder, mixing until smooth. Let cool for 5 minutes.

4   In a large bowl, whisk together the eggs and both sugars until combined. Add the sour cream, oil, and vanilla and whisk until well combined. Pour in the stout mixture and whisk until incorporated. Fold in the flour mixture using a rubber spatula and mix just until incorporated and no streaks of flour remain. Pour the batter into the prepared Bundt pan.

5   Bake for 40 to 45 minutes, rotating halfway through, until a toothpick inserted comes out clean with a few moist crumbs. Let cool in the pan for 35 minutes, then gently loosen it around the edges and flip onto a wire rack and let cool completely.

6   **For the Irish Cream Ganache:** Place the white chocolate in a large bowl.

7   In a saucepan over medium heat, bring the heavy cream to a boil, then immediately pour it over the chocolate. Let the mixture sit for 2 minutes undisturbed. Using a whisk, starting from the center and gradually working your way out toward the edges of the bowl, whisk until smooth and emulsified. Add the Bailey's Irish Cream and salt and stir to incorporate. Let the ganache cool slightly.

8   Pour the ganache over the cake, allowing it to drip down the sides of the cake. Let the ganache set for about 20 minutes before serving. Store any leftover cake, covered, in the fridge for up to 3 days.

CHOCOLATE CHIFFON CAKE

MAKES ONE 9 IN [23 CM] CAKE	
CHOCOLATE CHIFFON CAKE	
7	eggs
¾ cup [180 g]	hot coffee
½ cup [45 g]	Dutch-process cocoa powder
3 oz [85 g]	dark chocolate, finely chopped
1½ cups [190 g]	cake flour
2 tsp	baking powder
1 tsp	kosher salt
¼ tsp	baking soda
1¾ cups [350 g]	granulated sugar, divided
½ cup [115 g]	neutral oil
2 tsp	vanilla extract
½ tsp	cream of tartar
CHOCOLATE WHIPPED CREAM	
5 oz [140 g]	60% dark chocolate, chopped
1¾ cups [420 g]	heavy cream
¼ cup [30 g]	confectioners' sugar, sifted

This cake is a tribute to the popular chiffon cakes you find at most Asian bakeries. Impossibly fluffy from a cloud of whipped egg whites, its sky-high profile is beautiful to behold. The texture is between an angel food cake and a sponge cake, striking the balance between airy and moist. Paired with light and delicate chocolate whipped cream, this cake is not too sweet and not too heavy. What makes this chiffon unique is the addition of melted chocolate—just enough to add an extra punch of chocolatey goodness while still maintaining the integrity of the delicate and airy texture of the chiffon cake.

DIRECTIONS

1 **For the Chocolate Chiffon Cake:** Separate the egg yolks and egg whites into two small bowls, and let come to room temperature for about 30 minutes. (Room-temperature egg whites will be airier and more voluminous when whipped, so don't skip this step.)

2 Preheat the oven to 325°F [160°C]. You will need an ungreased 9 in [23 cm] (16-cup [3.8 L] capacity) tube pan. (The ungreased tube pan will allow the cake to "climb" up the sides as it bakes.)

3 In a small bowl or glass measuring cup, pour the coffee over the cocoa powder and add in the chopped chocolate. Stir until the chocolate is completely melted. Set aside and allow to cool slightly. →

4   In a medium bowl, sift together the flour, baking powder, salt, and baking soda. Set aside.

5   In a large mixing bowl, whisk together the egg yolks and 1 cup [200 g] of the granulated sugar until combined. Add the oil and vanilla and mix until well combined, about 1 minute. Next, add in the melted chocolate mixture and mix until well combined.

6   Add the sifted flour mixture to the yolk mixture and stir just until combined, scraping down the bowl as needed.

7   In a separate large bowl using a hand mixer or in the bowl of a stand mixer fitted with the whisk attachment, beat the egg whites and cream of tartar on medium speed. Once the egg whites start to get foamy, gradually stream in the remaining ¾ cup [150 g] of granulated sugar and beat just until stiff, glossy peaks form. Take care not to overbeat. Using a rubber spatula, gently fold in one third of the egg whites into the batter, then continue with the remaining batter. Fold just until blended and no streaks remain, taking care not to deflate the eggs.

8   Pour the batter into the ungreased tube pan and run a butter knife or chopstick through the batter to remove any bubbles. Smooth the top with an offset spatula and bake for 55 to 60 minutes or until the center springs back and a wooden skewer comes out clean. Immediately invert the tube pan onto a wire rack and let cool completely upside down, about 1 hour.

9   To remove the cake from the pan, run a knife around the inside of the tube pan and the center core to help loosen. Invert onto a cake stand or turntable and remove the pan.

10   **For the Chocolate Whipped Cream:** Add the chopped chocolate to a heatproof bowl. In a small saucepan over medium heat, bring the heavy cream to a boil. Pour over the chopped chocolate and whisk until homogeneous. Cover and chill in the refrigerator for at least 2 hours or overnight. Add the confectioners' sugar and whip the chocolate cream with a hand mixer or in a stand mixer fitted with the whisk attachment until light and soft peaks form.

11   Spread the whipped cream over the top, sides, and inside of the chiffon cake using an offset spatula. Chill in the refrigerator for 30 minutes prior to serving. Store any leftover cake, covered, in the fridge for up to 3 days.

GO-TO CHOCOLATE CAKE

MAKES ONE 8 IN [20 CM] TWO-LAYER CAKE	
CHOCOLATE CAKE	
1 cup [85 g]	Dutch-process cocoa powder
1 cup [240 g]	hot coffee
2 cups [250 g]	all-purpose flour
1 cup [200 g]	granulated sugar
1 cup [200 g]	light brown sugar, packed
2 tsp	baking soda
1 tsp	baking powder
1 tsp	kosher salt
1 cup [240 g]	buttermilk, well shaken, or sour cream, at room temperature
½ cup [115 g]	neutral oil
½ cup [115 g]	unsalted butter, melted
2	large eggs, at room temperature
2 tsp	vanilla extract
SWISS MERINGUE BUTTERCREAM	
½ cup [120 g]	egg whites (from 3 or 4 large eggs)
1 cup plus 2 Tbsp [225 g]	granulated sugar
1½ cups [340 g]	unsalted butter, cubed, at room temperature
2 tsp	vanilla bean paste or extract
¼ tsp	kosher salt
8 oz [225 g]	60% to 70% dark chocolate, chopped

Chocolate cake is synonymous with birthdays, celebrations, and milestones, so it's imperative that everyone has a no-fail, go-to chocolate cake in their back pocket. This one is mine. Adapted from the iconic Hershey's Black Magic cake that I grew up on, I've fine-tuned it to absolute perfection. It's quick and uses pantry staples, making it ideal for busy weeknights or last-minute gatherings. Not to mention it's incredibly forgiving and extremely versatile. I have used it to make sheet cakes, Bundt cakes, and cupcakes, and it works well with any of your favorite frostings. I like to use my go-to: Swiss meringue buttercream. An absolute workhorse in the world of frostings, Swiss meringue buttercream is the unsung hero and will always be my preferred frosting due to its remarkable stability and silky-smooth texture.

DIRECTIONS

1 **For the Chocolate Cake:** Preheat the oven to 350°F [175°C]. Grease the bottoms of two 8 in [20 cm] round cake pans and line with parchment paper.

2 In a small bowl or large glass measuring cup, add the cocoa powder and hot coffee and stir until well combined and smooth. Set aside to allow the cocoa powder to bloom.

3 In the bowl of a stand mixer fitted with the paddle attachment, combine the flour, both sugars, baking soda, baking powder, and salt and mix on low until evenly distributed. $\longrightarrow$

4 In a medium bowl, whisk together the buttermilk, oil, butter, eggs, and vanilla. With the mixer running on low, carefully add the wet ingredients to the flour mixture and mix for 1 minute. Scrape down the sides and bottom of the bowl with a rubber spatula to ensure there are no dry patches. Turn the mixer back on low and slowly pour in the coffee mixture and mix just until combined. Scrape down the bowl once more to ensure everything is incorporated and no dry patches remain. The batter will be quite runny.

5 Pour the batter into the prepared cake pan and smooth the top with an offset spatula. Bake for 35 to 40 minutes or until a toothpick comes out clean and the center reads an internal temperature of 205°F [95°C].

6 Transfer the pan to a wire rack and allow the cake to cool completely in the pan before frosting.

7 **For the Swiss Meringue Buttercream:** Fill a large saucepan with 1 in [2.5 cm] of water and bring to a gentle simmer over medium heat.

8 In a large heatproof bowl large enough to fit over the saucepan without touching the water, combine the egg whites and sugar. Whisk until combined. Place the bowl over the simmering pan of water and, whisking constantly, heat the egg mixture until it reaches 165°F [75°C] and the sugar is completely dissolved.

9 Remove the bowl from the heat and transfer the egg mixture to the bowl of a stand mixer fitted with the whisk attachment. Beat on medium speed until stiff peaks form and the sides of the bowl are cool to the touch, 5 to 7 minutes.

10 Add the butter (yes, all at once!), vanilla, and salt and mix on low speed for 10 to 15 minutes, until completely incorporated and homogeneous. It may begin to look curdled, but don't panic and give it time. In the meantime, melt the chocolate over the double boiler used to cook the egg white mixture (see page 14). Set aside and let cool slightly.

11 Switch to the paddle attachment and mix on low speed for another 10 minutes (the paddle will help remove any air bubbles). Add the cooled melted chocolate and mix until fully incorporated.

12 **To Assemble:** Trim and level the tops of the cooled cakes if needed. Freeze the cake layers for about 15 minutes to make them easier to frost.

13 Arrange the first cake layer cut-side up on a turntable. Spread the buttercream on top and evenly distribute using an offset spatula. Stack the next cake layer on top. Frost the top and sides of the cake with the remaining frosting. Use a cake scraper to clean up any gaps and create a smooth finish. Transfer the cake to a cake stand to serve. Store, covered, in the fridge for up to 3 days.

GÂTEAU CONCORDE

MAKES ONE 8 IN [20 CM] CAKE	
CHOCOLATE MERINGUE	
1¼ cups [150 g]	confectioners' sugar, sifted
6 Tbsp [30 g]	Dutch-process cocoa powder
5	large egg whites, at room temperature
¾ cup [150 g]	granulated sugar
CRÈME FRAÎCHE MOUSSE	
6 oz [170 g]	60% dark chocolate, chopped
1½ cups [360 g]	heavy cream, divided
⅓ cup [80 g]	crème fraîche
Confectioners' sugar, for dusting	

The Gâteau Concorde, a.k.a. Concord Cake, is a true gem. Legendary French pastry chef Gaston Lenôtre created this dessert to celebrate the launch of the Concorde aircraft in the early 1970s while he was designing menus for Air France, and the cake has since been modified and recreated by chefs around the world. I first discovered this beauty in pastry school and immediately fell in love with its alluring appearance, texture, and flavor. It remains one of my most memorable bakes from pastry school. The cake features layers of crispy, chewy chocolate meringue that are smothered in a luscious chocolate mousse, resulting in contrasting textures that are light yet decadent. The cake is decorated with sticks of meringue, producing a show-stopping dessert worthy of any holiday or special celebration.

DIRECTIONS

1 **For the Chocolate Meringue:** Prep the piping guide for the meringue discs by tracing two 7 in [18 cm] circles on a piece of parchment paper. Line one baking sheet with the guide face down and another with a blank piece of parchment paper.

2 In a medium bowl, sift together the confectioners' sugar and cocoa powder.

3 In the bowl of a stand mixer fitted with the whisk attachment or in a large bowl with a hand mixer, whip the egg whites on medium speed until frothy. Gradually add the granulated sugar and whip until you've reached glossy, stiff peaks. Gently fold in the cocoa powder mixture until no streaks remain, taking care not to deflate the egg whites. →

4   Transfer the meringue to a pastry bag fitted with a ½ in [13 mm] round tip. Using the guides, pipe the meringue into two 7 in [18 cm] circles, starting from the center and working your way out. On the other baking sheet, pipe the remaining meringue into 8 in [20 cm] long logs, leaving about 1 in [2.5 cm] between each. Let the meringue sit for 30 minutes at room temperature. Meanwhile, preheat the oven to 250°F [120°C].

5   Bake the meringue for 45 to 50 minutes, until firm and crisp. To check, you should be able to release the meringue off the parchment with an offset spatula. Transfer the meringue to wire racks to cool completely.

6   **For the Crème Fraîche Mousse:** Place the chocolate in a large bowl.

7   In a small saucepan over medium heat, bring 1 cup [240 g] of the cream to a boil. Immediately pour it over the chopped chocolate and let sit for 1 minute, undisturbed, then whisk until smooth and emulsified. Cool the mixture completely and refrigerate for at least 2 hours.

8   In the bowl of a stand mixer fitted with the whisk attachment or in a large bowl with a hand mixer, combine the chocolate mixture, the remaining ½ cup [120 g] of heavy cream, and the crème fraîche. Whip on medium speed until soft peaks form.

9   Place a meringue disc in the center of a cake stand. Spoon half of the chocolate mousse on top of the disc and smooth with an offset spatula. Place the other meringue disc on top and repeat with the remaining mousse. Refrigerate for at least 2 hours to set.

10   To finish, break the meringue logs into pieces that are about the same height as the cake. Arrange them vertically around the perimeter of the cake, lightly pressing each piece into the cream to help stick. Cover the top with broken pieces. Refrigerate the cake for at least 4 hours or overnight for the best flavor and texture.

11   Dust with confectioners' sugar and serve. Store the cake, covered, in the fridge for up to 3 days.

TWICE-BAKED CHOCOLATE TAHINI BLACKBERRY CAKE

MAKES ONE 9 IN [23 CM] CAKE	
½ cup [115 g]	unsalted butter, cubed
8 oz [225 g]	60% to 70% dark chocolate, chopped
½ cup [45 g]	Dutch-process cocoa powder, plus more for dusting
½ cup [130 g]	tahini, well stirred
2 tsp	vanilla extract
½ tsp	kosher salt
7	eggs, separated, at room temperature
1¼ cups [250 g]	granulated sugar, divided
⅓ cup [110 g]	seedless blackberry jam
Crème fraîche, for serving	

As the name suggests, this flourless cake is baked twice, which produces two distinct layers and textures: the bottom layer has a fudgy, brownie-like consistency and the top layer a molten, mousse-like consistency. The juxtaposition between the two is simply perfection. The cake is deceptively simple as it uses just a few ingredients and both layers use the same batter. This ingenious recipe comes from *Food & Wine*, and I've transformed it into a chocolate-tahini affair. I also like to hide a thin swirl of blackberry jam between the layers for a welcome surprise to balance the richness of the chocolate. The bold flavor will have even the most discerning chocolate lover singing its praises, making this the perfect dessert candidate for a dinner party.

DIRECTIONS

1   Preheat the oven to 350°F [175°C]. Grease a 9 in [23 cm] springform pan and line the bottom and sides with parchment paper.

2   Gently melt the butter and dark chocolate over a double boiler (see page 14). Once melted, remove from the heat, then stir in the cocoa powder, tahini, vanilla, and salt and set aside to cool.

3   In the bowl of a stand mixer fitted with the whisk attachment or in a large bowl using an electric mixer, whisk together the egg yolks and ¾ cup [150 g] of the sugar until light and fluffy, about 2 minutes. Set aside.

4   In a medium bowl using clean beaters, whisk the egg whites on medium speed until frothy. Gradually stream in the remaining ½ cup [100 g] of sugar and whip to soft, glossy peaks, taking care not to overbeat.

5   Gently fold the melted chocolate mixture into the reserved egg yolk mixture just until combined. Gently fold in the egg whites in three additions, just until no streaks remain.

6   Carefully spoon one-third of the batter into a storage container, cover with a lid, and refrigerate until ready to use. This will be the molten top layer.   →

7 Pour the remaining two-thirds of the cake batter into the prepared springform pan and smooth the top with an offset spatula. Bake for 25 to 30 minutes or until a toothpick inserted in the center comes out clean. Let the cake cool in the pan on a wire rack for about 30 minutes. Remove the remaining batter from the fridge and set aside.

8 Gently warm the jam in a small saucepan over low heat just until loosened and spreadable.

9 Once the cake is cool, spread the blackberry jam in an even layer over the cake, leaving a ⅛ in [3 mm] border around the edges, ensuring the jam doesn't directly touch the cake pan. Spread the reserved batter over the jam and smooth the top with an offset spatula. Bake for another 17 to 22 minutes or until the edges have set and the center has a slight jiggle.

10 Transfer the pan to a wire rack and let the cake cool in the pan. Remove the cake from the pan and dust the top with cocoa powder. Slice and serve the cake with a dollop of crème fraîche. This cake is best served the day it is made but can be wrapped and stored in the refrigerator for up to 3 days.

CHOCOLATE BURNT BASQUE CHEESECAKE

MAKES ONE 8 IN [20 CM] CHEESECAKE	
6 oz [170 g]	70% bittersweet chocolate, chopped
1¼ cups [300 g]	heavy cream
24 oz [680 g]	cream cheese
½ cup [100 g]	granulated sugar
½ cup [100 g]	light brown sugar, packed
1 tsp	vanilla extract
½ tsp	kosher salt
4	eggs, at room temperature
3 Tbsp	Dutch-process cocoa powder
3 Tbsp	all-purpose flour

NOTE ○ Make sure to use a deep dish springform pan. You can also make the cheesecake in a food processor. Starting with step 4, follow the mixing method in step 4 on page 95, then add the sifted cocoa and flour at the end.

Some recipes are born to be great, and the Basque cheesecake is just one example. The highly praised cheesecake was created by Chef Santiago Rivera at La Viña in San Sebastian and has generated fierce discussion and intrigue. I decided to adapt this magical recipe into a chocolate version. Surrounded by ruffles of parchment paper, it has a slightly cracked and sunken, blackened top. Inside you will discover a soft, custardy, molten center reminiscent of Camembert cheese. Despite its appearance, it is deceptively simple to make and breaks all the rules of a traditional cheesecake: There's no graham cracker crust, it bakes at a high temperature, and it doesn't require a water bath. As soon as you take a bite, this incredibly rich and decadent cheesecake, with its creamy, melt-in-your mouth texture, will make you want to Basque in all its glory.

DIRECTIONS

1 Preheat the oven at 475°F [245°C] for at least 30 minutes to ensure the oven is sufficiently hot when you put the cheesecake in. Fit an 8 in [20 cm] round springform pan, 3 in [8 cm] deep, with two pieces of parchment paper, leaving a 2 in [5 cm] overhang folded down over the sides of the pan. I like to crumple the paper into a ball to make it more pliable, then spread one piece of parchment into the pan and fit the second piece on top. Smooth out the paper to ensure it's fitted in the pan. It's okay if the paper isn't completely smooth along the sides.

2 Place the chopped chocolate in a large heatproof bowl.

3 In a small saucepan over medium-low heat, bring the heavy cream just to a boil, then pour it over the chopped chocolate. Let sit for 3 minutes, then whisk until smooth and the chocolate is completely melted. Set aside and let cool slightly. →

4 In a stand mixer fitted with the paddle attachment, beat the cream cheese, both sugars, vanilla, and salt on medium speed. Scrape down the bowl, then add the eggs one at a time, until incorporated. Scrape down the bowl and beat until no lumps remain. Add the melted chocolate and beat on low speed until combined. Sift in the cocoa powder and flour and mix until incorporated. Scrape down the bowl until no streaks remain.

5 Carefully pour the batter into the prepared pan and bake for 35 to 40 minutes. The top should be dark and the center should still be very jiggly. It will look unset and liquidy, but that's what we're after. Let cool in the pan on a wire rack for 1 hour, then transfer to the refrigerator until completely cool.

6 Remove the cheesecake from the pan and gently peel the parchment paper away from the exterior. Serve at room temperature. Store any leftover cake, covered, in the fridge for up to 3 days.

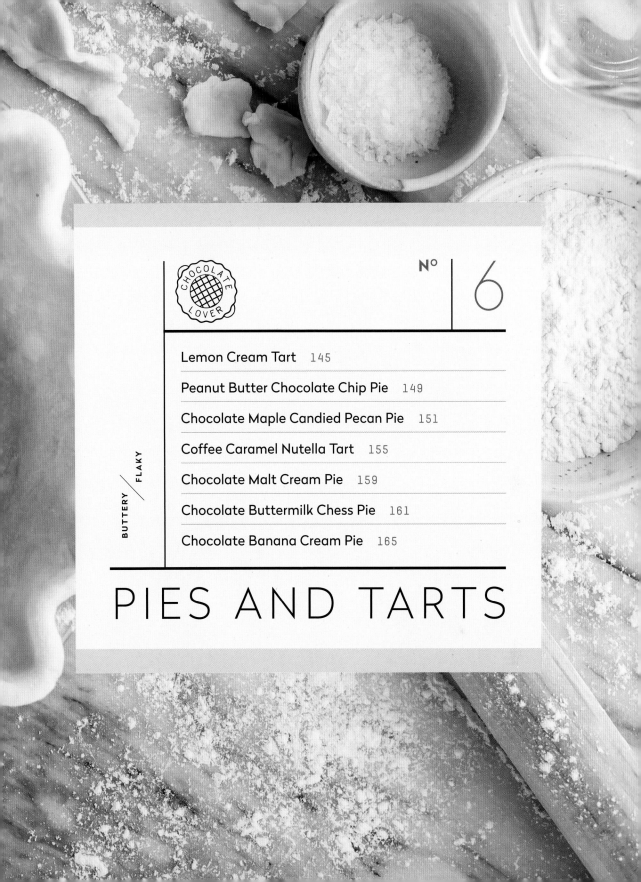

CHOCOLATE LOVER

Nº 6

BUTTERY / FLAKY

Lemon Cream Tart   145

Peanut Butter Chocolate Chip Pie   149

Chocolate Maple Candied Pecan Pie   151

Coffee Caramel Nutella Tart   155

Chocolate Malt Cream Pie   159

Chocolate Buttermilk Chess Pie   161

Chocolate Banana Cream Pie   165

PIES AND TARTS

LEMON CREAM TART

ONE 9 IN [23 CM] TART	
WHITE CHOCOLATE–LEMON CREAM	
7 oz [200 g]	white chocolate, chopped
½ cup [100 g]	granulated sugar
3 Tbsp	lemon zest
5	large eggs
1 cup [240 g]	freshly squeezed lemon juice (about 6 lemons)
¼ tsp	kosher salt
½ cup [115 g]	unsalted butter, at room temperature
PÂTE BRISÉE	
1¼ cups [156 g]	all-purpose flour
2 tsp	granulated sugar
½ tsp	kosher salt
7 Tbsp [100 g]	cold unsalted butter, cubed
1 to 2 Tbsp	ice water
Edible flowers, for decoration	
WHITE CHOCOLATE CHANTILLY	
4 oz [115 g]	white chocolate, chopped
1 cup [240 g]	cold heavy cream, divided
1 Tbsp	granulated sugar

White chocolate is often criticized for being cloyingly sweet, yet it's this very quality that makes it an ideal match for tart lemon desserts. With this in mind, I was inspired to recreate my favorite lemon cream tart by the renowned pastry chef Pierre Herme. I leveraged the sweetness of the chocolate along with its cocoa butter content to cut down on the sugar and butter in the original recipe, striking the perfect balance and resulting in an ethereal texture that is simply irresistible. To guarantee a creamy texture, I use white chocolate that has a higher cocoa butter content, such as Valrhona, Callebaut, Cocoa Barry, or Green and Blacks. I dare you to not eat all the cream by the spoonful.

DIRECTIONS

1 **For the White Chocolate–Lemon Cream:** In a large heatproof bowl, add the chopped white chocolate and set aside.

2 In a small bowl, combine the sugar with the lemon zest and rub together to release the oils from the zest.

3 Fill a medium saucepan with about 1 in [2.5 cm] of water and bring to a gentle simmer over medium heat.

4 In a large metal bowl, whisk the eggs. While slowly whisking the eggs, gradually pour in the sugar mixture followed by the lemon juice and salt. Whisk until combined. →

5 Place the bowl over the saucepan of simmering water, ensuring the bottom of the bowl is not directly touching the water. Whisk constantly until the lemon cream has thickened and reaches 180°F [82°C], 7 to 10 minutes. To remove any uncooked eggs, strain the lemon cream through a fine-mesh sieve into the bowl with the white chocolate.

6 Let sit for 5 minutes, then vigorously whisk to combine, ensuring the chocolate is completely melted. Continue to let cool slightly to 140°F [60°C].

7 Use an immersion blender on high speed to blend the mixture. Make sure the blender is submerged in the lemon cream, otherwise it will splatter everywhere. Add the butter a few Tbsp at a time and blend for 1 to 2 minutes to ensure the butter is fully incorporated and completely emulsified. There should be no remaining chunks or streaks of butter, and the lemon cream should be pale yellow and silky smooth. Alternatively, you can do this process in a regular blender.

8 Press a piece of plastic wrap directly onto the surface of the cream and refrigerate for at least 4 hours, or ideally overnight.

9 **For the Pâte Brisée:** In the bowl of a stand mixer fitted with the paddle attachment, mix together the flour, sugar, and salt on low speed until combined. Add the cubed butter all at once and mix on low speed until the mixture resembles the texture of almond meal, 3 to 5 minutes. Add the ice water and mix just until it starts to come together. Do not be tempted to add more water than called for.

10 Transfer the dough to a lightly floured surface and shape into a round disc. Wrap in plastic wrap and refrigerate for at least 1 hour.

11 Preheat the oven to 350°F [175°C]. Unwrap the dough, roll it out into an 11 in [28 cm] circle, and fit it into a 9 in [23 cm] tart pan, pressing it into the bottom and up the sides and trimming the edges with a sharp knife. Dock the bottom of the tart crust with a fork. Take a piece of parchment paper big enough to line the tart shell and crumple it up into a ball to make it more pliable. Smooth out the ball of parchment paper, fit it into the tart shell, and fill with uncooked rice, dried beans, or pie weights. Blind bake for 20 minutes (this will prevent the tart shell from shrinking). Remove the pie weights and parchment paper and bake for another 10 to 15 minutes or until golden brown and fully cooked. Let cool completely on a wire rack.

12 **For the White Chocolate Chantilly:**
Add the chopped white chocolate to a
medium heatproof bowl.

13 In a small saucepan, bring ½ cup [120 g]
of the heavy cream to a gentle simmer over
medium heat, then pour over the white
chocolate. Let sit undisturbed for 2 minutes,
then whisk until smooth and the white
chocolate is completely melted. Refrigerate
the mixture for at least 4 hours or overnight.

14 In the bowl of a stand mixer fitted with
the whisk attachment, combine the remaining
½ cup [120 g] of heavy cream and the cooled
white chocolate. Whip on medium speed until
soft peaks form, 2 to 4 minutes.

15 **To Assemble:** Spread the lemon cream into
the cooled tart shell and smooth the top using
an offset spatula. Top the lemon tart with the
Chantilly. For a beautiful decoration, transfer the
cream into a pastry bag and use a St. Honore
pastry tip to make squiggles or use a round
pastry tip for dollops. Top with edible flowers for
decoration. The tart is best served cold, so keep
covered in the refrigerator until ready to serve.
Cover any leftovers and store in the fridge for up
to 3 days.

PEANUT BUTTER CHOCOLATE CHIP PIE

MAKES ONE 9 IN [23 CM] PIE	
PIE CRUST	
½ cup [115 g]	unsalted butter, cubed
¼ cup [60 g]	ice water, or more as needed
1¼ cups [156 g]	all-purpose flour, plus more for dusting
1 Tbsp	granulated sugar
¼ tsp	kosher salt
1	egg, beaten, for the egg wash
CHOCOLATE CHIP COOKIE FILLING	
2	large eggs
1	large egg yolk
¾ cup [150 g]	light brown sugar, packed
¼ cup [50 g]	granulated sugar
1 tsp	vanilla extract
½ cup [65 g]	all-purpose flour
¼ tsp	kosher salt
½ cup [115 g]	unsalted butter, cubed, at room temperature
½ cup [130 g]	creamy peanut butter
¾ cup [130 g]	semisweet chocolate chips, plus more for sprinkling (optional)

Chocolate chip pie is a classic dessert that never fails to please. Based on the iconic Nestlé Toll House recipe, I've transformed this classic pie into a peanut butter version. The result is a perfectly soft, gooey, and chewy pie that's packed with melt-in-your-mouth chocolate morsels. Admittedly, whenever I bake this pie, I can't help but think of the episode of *Friends* where Phoebe's grandma's secret chocolate chip cookie recipe is revealed to be the one on the back of the Nestlé Toll House bag. While this pie may not be a closely guarded family secret, the addition of peanut butter will make this chocolate chip pie a standout dessert that will have everyone asking for the recipe.

DIRECTIONS

1 **For the Pie Crust:** Chill the butter and ice water separately in the freezer for 10 minutes to get extra cold.

2 In the bowl of a stand mixer fitted with the paddle attachment, add the flour, sugar, and salt and mix on low speed to combine. Add the butter and mix on low speed for 15 seconds until the pieces of butter are the size of walnut halves. With the mixer running on low speed, gradually pour in the ice water and mix for another 30 to 60 seconds, just until the dough starts to come together, taking care not to overmix. The dough should be shaggy, with visible chunks of butter. If needed, add 1 Tbsp more ice water. $\longrightarrow$

3   Transfer the dough to a lightly floured work surface and shape it into a disc. Wrap in plastic wrap and refrigerate for at least 1 hour or overnight. Refrigerated dough, tightly wrapped in plastic wrap, can be stored for up to 2 days. To make ahead, wrap the dough in plastic wrap and a layer of aluminum foil and freeze for up to 1 month. Then thaw in the fridge 1 day before you plan to bake.

4   Preheat the oven to 425°F [220°C].

5   On a lightly floured work surface, roll the dough into an 11 in [28 cm] circle and transfer to a 9 in [23 cm] pie plate. Trim the edges with kitchen scissors or a sharp knife, leaving a ½ in [13 mm] overhang around the edge. Tuck the excess dough under itself and crimp all around to seal the edges of the pie dough. Dock the bottom of the pie shell with a fork to prevent the dough from puffing up while it bakes. Chill the prepared pie crust in the refrigerator for 15 minutes prior to baking (this allows the gluten to relax, which prevents shrinking, and also lets the butter firm up, which gives us those flaky layers, so don't skip this step!).

6   Take a piece of parchment paper big enough to line the pie shell and crumple it up into a ball to make it more pliable. Smooth out the ball of parchment paper, fit it into the pie shell, and fill with uncooked rice, dried beans, or pie weights.

7   Bake for 15 to 20 minutes, until the edges start to set. Remove the crust from the oven and carefully lift the corners of the parchment

paper to remove it along with the weights. In a small bowl, combine the beaten egg with 1 Tbsp of water and brush the bottom of the pie crust with a thin layer of this egg wash. Return the crust to the oven and bake for 2 to 3 more minutes, until the bottom is set and light golden brown in color. Let the crust cool completely on a wire rack.

8   Preheat the oven to 325°F [160°C].

9   **For the Chocolate Chip Cookie Filling:** In a stand mixer fitted with the whisk attachment, whip the eggs and egg yolk on high for 5 minutes until light and frothy. Add both sugars and the vanilla and mix for 1 minute on medium speed. Scrape down the bowl and add the flour and salt and mix on low until well combined. Add the butter and peanut butter and mix on medium-low for another 1 minute until well combined. Fold in the chocolate chips, being careful not to overmix. The mixture should be the consistency of cake batter.

10   Spoon the filling into the parbaked pie shell and top with more chocolate chips, if using. Bake for 50 to 60 minutes or until a toothpick inserted in the center comes out clean. Transfer the pie to a wire rack and let cool. Store tightly wrapped, at room temperature, for up to 3 days.

CHOCOLATE MAPLE CANDIED PECAN PIE

MAKES ONE 9 IN [23 CM] PIE	
PIE CRUST	
½ cup [115 g]	unsalted butter, cubed
¼ cup [60 g]	ice water, or more as needed
1¼ cups [156 g]	all-purpose flour
1 Tbsp	granulated sugar
¼ tsp	kosher salt
1	egg, beaten, for the egg wash
CANDIED PECANS	
1½ cups [170 g]	pecan halves
2 Tbsp	dark brown sugar, packed
2 Tbsp	unsalted butter
1 Tbsp	maple syrup
CHOCOLATE PECAN PIE FILLING	
6 Tbsp [85 g]	unsalted butter, cubed
4	large eggs, at room temperature
¾ cup [150 g]	dark brown sugar, packed
½ cup [170 g]	light corn syrup
¼ cup [80 g]	maple syrup
1 Tbsp	bourbon
1 tsp	vanilla extract
½ tsp	kosher salt
3 oz [85 g]	60% dark chocolate, chopped

Chocolate pecan pie is a long-standing family favorite that's not reserved exclusively for Thanksgiving; it's on a monthly rotation in my household. The secret to my perfect version lies in the ingredients since the list is so simple: candied pecans, maple syrup, bourbon, and brown butter. I like to candy the nuts in sugar so they have a toasted, caramelized flavor that can stand on its own. I also use a mix of maple syrup for flavor and corn syrup for that distinct gooey texture. It's imperative you use real maple syrup here; the knock-off stuff won't do. I prefer to chop the chocolate instead of melting it so it doesn't overshadow all the flavors. This pie is truly much greater than the sum of its parts and is now what my family claims as the best chocolate pecan pie.

DIRECTIONS

1 **For the Pie Crust:** Chill the butter and ice water separately in the freezer for 10 minutes to get extra cold.

2 In the bowl of a stand mixer fitted with the paddle attachment, add the flour, sugar, and salt and mix on low speed to combine. Add the butter and mix on low speed for 15 seconds until the pieces of butter are the size of walnut halves. With the mixer running on low speed, gradually pour in the ice water and mix for another 30 to 60 seconds, just until the dough starts to come together, taking care not to overmix. The dough should be shaggy, with visible chunks of butter. If needed, add 1 Tbsp more ice water. $\longrightarrow$

3 Transfer the dough to a lightly floured work surface and shape it into a disc. Wrap in plastic wrap and refrigerate for at least 1 hour or overnight. Refrigerated dough tightly wrapped in plastic wrap can be stored for up to 2 days. To make ahead, wrap the dough in plastic wrap and a layer of aluminum foil and freeze for up to 1 month. Then thaw in the fridge 1 day before you plan to bake.

4 Preheat the oven to 425°F [220°C].

5 On a lightly floured work surface, roll the dough into an 11 in [28 cm] circle and transfer to a 9 in [23 cm] pie plate. Trim the edges with kitchen scissors or a sharp knife, leaving a ½ in [13 mm] overhang around the edge. Tuck the excess dough under itself and crimp all around to seal the edges of the pie dough. Dock the bottom of the pie shell with a fork to prevent the dough from puffing up while it bakes. Chill the prepared pie crust in the refrigerator for 15 minutes prior to baking (this allows the gluten to relax, which prevents shrinking, and also lets the butter firm up, which gives us those flaky layers, so don't skip this step!).

6 Take a piece of parchment paper big enough to line the pie shell and crumple it up into a ball to make it more pliable. Smooth out the ball of parchment paper, fit it into the pie shell, and fill with uncooked rice, dried beans, or pie weights.

7 Bake for 15 to 20 minutes, until the edges start to set. Remove the crust from the oven and carefully lift the corners of the parchment paper to remove it along with the weights. In a small bowl, combine the beaten egg with 1 Tbsp of water and brush the bottom of the pie crust with a thin layer of this egg wash. Return the crust to the oven and bake for 2 to 3 more minutes, until the bottom is set and light golden brown in color. Let the crust cool completely on a wire rack.

8 **For the Candied Pecans:** Lower the oven temperature to 350°F [175°C].

9 On a parchment paper–lined baking sheet, toast the pecans in the oven until fragrant, 5 to 7 minutes. Remove from the oven and roughly chop the toasted pecans into bite-size pieces. Reserve the baking sheet.

10 In a large skillet over medium heat, combine the brown sugar, butter, and maple syrup and cook just until melted and bubbly. Add the pecans and stir to coat until the sugar mixture is evenly distributed.

11 Spread the candied pecans onto the reserved baking sheet to cool completely. $\longrightarrow$

12 **For the Chocolate Pecan Pie Filling:** In a wide skillet over medium-low heat, brown the butter, whisking constantly, 5 to 7 minutes. Once the milk solids look toasted and the butter turns a golden color, transfer to a bowl, scraping all the milk solids from the skillet along with the melted butter. Set aside to cool slightly.

13 In a large mixing bowl, beat together the eggs, brown sugar, corn syrup, and maple syrup until well combined, about 2 minutes. Stir in the cooled brown butter, bourbon, vanilla, and salt. Let the mixture rest for at least 10 minutes.

14 Distribute the cooled candied pecans and chopped chocolate into the parbaked pie shell and spread in an even layer, then carefully pour the filling into the crust.

15 Transfer the pie pan onto a baking sheet and bake for 40 to 50 minutes, until the center is set. Cover the edges of the pie crust with foil if the crust starts to brown before the center is set.

16 Remove the pie from the oven and cool completely on a wire rack before serving. Store any leftovers, tightly wrapped, in the refrigerator for up to 3 days.

COFFEE CARAMEL NUTELLA TART

MAKES ONE 9 IN [23 CM] TART	
HAZELNUT PÂTE BRISÉE	
1 cup [125 g]	all-purpose flour, plus more for dusting
¼ cup [25 g]	hazelnut flour (see Note)
2 tsp	granulated sugar
½ tsp	kosher salt
7 Tbsp [100 g]	cold unsalted butter, cubed
1 to 2 Tbsp	ice water
COFFEE CARAMEL	
½ cup [120 g]	heavy cream, plus more as needed
2 tsp	espresso powder
1 cup [200 g]	granulated sugar
1 Tbsp	light corn syrup or honey
½ cup [115 g]	unsalted butter, cubed
1 tsp	vanilla extract
1 tsp	kosher salt
NUTELLA GANACHE	
4 oz [115 g]	60% dark chocolate, finely chopped
½ cup [120 g]	heavy cream
¼ tsp	kosher salt
½ cup [130 g]	Nutella
Flaky sea salt, for sprinkling	

NOTE ○ If you can't find hazelnut flour, you can substitute almond flour or all-purpose flour.

It's rare to find something that is truly perfect, but this tart just might be one of those things. Thanks to Claudia Fleming, author of *The Last Course* and former pastry chef at Gramercy Tavern, the iconic caramel chocolate tart has become forever immortalized in the pastry world. While not trying to mess with perfection, I've tweaked a few things and put my own twist on it. Including coffee, caramel, and hazelnut creates a heavenly combination and brings this ultimate indulgence to a new level. The creamy caramel filling is infused with espresso, which adds a bold and robust flavor. And the dark chocolate Nutella ganache adds a faint yet deliciously nutty undertone. One taste, and you'll understand why this famous tart is a must-try for any chocolate lover.

DIRECTIONS

1 **For the Hazelnut Pâte Brisée:** In the bowl of a stand mixer fitted with the paddle attachment, mix together both flours, the sugar, and salt on low speed until combined. Add the cubed butter all at once and mix on low speed until the mixture resembles coarse sand, 3 to 5 minutes. Add the ice water and mix just until it starts to come together. Do not be tempted to add more water than called for.

2 Transfer the dough to a lightly floured surface and shape into a round disc. Wrap in plastic wrap and refrigerate for at least 1 hour.

3 Preheat the oven to 350°F [175°C]. →

4 Roll the dough into an 11 in [28 cm] circle and carefully fit it into a 9 in [23 cm] tart pan, pressing it into the bottom and up the sides and trimming the edges with a sharp knife. Prick the bottom of the tart crust with a fork. Take a piece of parchment paper big enough to line the tart shell and crumple it up into a ball to make it more pliable. Smooth out the ball of parchment paper, fit it into the tart shell, and fill with uncooked rice, dried beans, or pie weights. This will prevent the tart shell from shrinking.

5 Blind bake for 20 minutes. Remove the parchment paper filled with the pie weights, then bake for another 10 to 15 minutes or until golden brown and fully cooked. Let cool completely on a wire rack.

6 **For the Coffee Caramel:** In a small saucepan over medium heat, bring the heavy cream to a boil. Remove from the heat, add the espresso powder, and cover the saucepan with plastic wrap to steep and infuse the cream for 10 minutes. Set aside.

7 In a clean medium saucepan, add the sugar, corn syrup, and ¼ cup [60 g] of water. Using your index finger, gently incorporate the water into the sugar until the mixture resembles wet sand. Wet your hand and clean the sides of the saucepan to remove any remaining dry bits of sugar. Heat the sugar over medium heat until it turns a deep amber color, 10 to 15 minutes. Resist the urge to stir, as stirring will agitate the sugar crystals and cause the sugar to seize up. Once the caramel reaches an amber

color, immediately remove from the heat and carefully add the butter and then the infused cream. Be careful of the steam as the caramel rapidly bubbles up and sputters.

8 Return the caramel to medium heat and cook, whisking constantly, until it reaches 238°F to 240°F [114°C to 115°C]. Remove from the heat and whisk in the vanilla and salt.

9 Pour the caramel into the tart shell and let cool completely, about 1 hour.

10 **For the Nutella Ganache:** Place the chopped chocolate into a large heatproof mixing bowl.

11 In a small saucepan over medium heat, bring the heavy cream to a boil, then immediately pour it over the chocolate. Let the mixture sit for 2 minutes undisturbed. Using a whisk, starting from the center and gradually working your way out toward the edges of the bowl, whisk until smooth and emulsified. Add the Nutella and whisk until fully incorporated. (For an extra smooth texture, use an immersion blender to emulsify.)

12 Pour the ganache over the caramel and smooth the top with an offset spatula, tilting the tart pan to help distribute it evenly. Allow the ganache to set, then sprinkle with flaky sea salt right before serving. Store any leftovers, tightly wrapped, in the refrigerator for up to 3 days.

CHOCOLATE MALT CREAM PIE

MAKES ONE 9 IN [23 CM] PIE	
CHOCOLATE COOKIE CRUST	
25	Oreo cookies, whole with filling
¼ tsp	kosher salt
5 Tbsp	unsalted butter, melted
CHOCOLATE PUDDING FILLING	
6 oz [170 g]	60% bittersweet chocolate, chopped
½ cup [100 g]	granulated sugar
¼ cup [32 g]	cornstarch
2 Tbsp	Dutch-process cocoa powder, sifted
2 cups [480 g]	whole milk
1 cup [240 g]	heavy cream
½ cup [60 g]	malted milk powder
½ tsp	kosher salt
2 tsp	vanilla extract
MALTED WHIPPED CREAM	
2 cups [480 g]	heavy cream
¼ cup [50 g]	granulated sugar
¼ cup [30 g]	malted milk powder
½ tsp	vanilla extract
Chocolate shavings, for decoration (optional)	

A slice of chocolate pudding pie instantly sends me back to my childhood and tugs on my heartstrings. I have an undying love and appreciation for those Jell-O pudding cups that I grew up on, so it's no surprise that chocolate pudding pie is one of my personal favorites. There's something so special about a cookie crumb crust, creamy pudding filling, and soft whipped cream. It just soothes the soul. Maybe it's the fact that this pie is easy to prepare since it uses cornstarch as a thickener instead of tempered eggs. Or maybe it's the malted whipped cream cloud and shaved chocolate curls on top. All I know is it's a guaranteed crowd-pleaser and is always welcomed with open arms at any potluck, gathering, or holiday.

DIRECTIONS

1 **For the Chocolate Cookie Crust:** Preheat the oven to 350°F [175°C].

2 In a food processor, process the Oreo cookies (whole, with the cream filling) into fine crumbs, then transfer to a medium bowl and stir in the salt. Pour the melted butter over the crumbs and stir until evenly moistened.

3 Pour the crumb mixture into a 9 in [23 cm] pie plate and press the mixture into the bottom and sides. Bake for 5 minutes, until fragrant and set. Let the crust cool completely on a wire rack. →

4 **For the Chocolate Pudding Filling:** Add the chopped chocolate to a large heatproof bowl and melt over a double boiler (see page 14). Once completely melted, remove from the heat and set aside.

5 In a small bowl, whisk together the sugar, cornstarch, and cocoa powder until combined.

6 In a medium saucepan, add the milk, heavy cream, malted milk powder, and salt and set over medium heat, whisking until the malted milk powder is fully dissolved. Once the milk starts to bubble and just come to a gentle simmer, whisk in the sugar mixture. While whisking constantly, bring to a boil for 2 minutes, until thickened. Remove from the heat and whisk in the melted chocolate and vanilla until smooth.

7 Pour the chocolate pudding into the cooled crust and cover with parchment paper placed directly on the surface to prevent a skin from forming. Refrigerate for 3 to 4 hours, until set.

8 **For the Malted Whipped Cream:** In a stand mixer fitted with the whisk attachment, combine the heavy cream, sugar, malted milk powder, and vanilla and whisk on medium-high speed just until soft peaks form or until it has reached your desired consistency, 3 to 4 minutes.

9 Spoon the whipped cream on top of the chilled pie and sprinkle with chocolate shavings, if using. Serve immediately. Store any leftovers, covered, in the refrigerator for up to 3 days.

CHOCOLATE BUTTERMILK CHESS PIE

MAKES ONE 9 IN [23 CM] PIE	
PIE CRUST	
½ cup [115 g]	unsalted butter, cubed
¼ cup [60 g]	buttermilk, or more as needed, well shaken
1¼ cups [156 g]	all-purpose flour
1 Tbsp	granulated sugar
¼ tsp	kosher salt
1	egg, beaten, for the egg wash
FILLING	
3 oz [85 g]	bittersweet chocolate, chopped
½ cup [115 g]	unsalted butter, cubed
2 Tbsp	Dutch-process cocoa powder
3	large eggs, at room temperature
1	large egg yolk, at room temperature
½ cup [100 g]	light brown sugar, packed
½ cup [100 g]	granulated sugar
2 Tbsp	all-purpose flour or finely ground cornmeal
½ tsp	kosher salt
¼ cup [60 g]	buttermilk, well shaken, at room temperature
1 tsp	vanilla extract
1 tsp	espresso powder (optional)
Whipped cream, for serving	
Chocolate shavings, for decoration	

Chocolate chess pie is pure, unadorned chocolate goodness and has remained a steadfast Southern favorite for good reason. My favorite part is the delicate, meringue-like crust that shatters when you cut into it. Hiding underneath the crackly crust lies a decadent, fudgy custard filling that reminds me of an underbaked brownie. The acid in the buttermilk helps balance the rich sweetness of the chocolate, and the espresso powder takes it to the next level. There's much debate about using cornmeal versus flour as the thickening agent, but I prefer flour to ensure a smooth filling and because I always have it in my pantry. If you prefer to keep it traditional, swap the flour for finely ground cornmeal.

DIRECTIONS

1 **For the Pie Crust:** Chill the butter and buttermilk separately in the freezer for 10 minutes to get extra cold.

2 In the bowl of a stand mixer fitted with the paddle attachment, add the flour, sugar, and salt and mix on low speed to combine. Add the butter and mix on low speed for 15 seconds until the pieces of butter are the size of walnut halves. With the mixer running on low speed, gradually pour in the buttermilk and mix for another 30 to 60 seconds, just until the dough starts to come together, taking care not to overmix. The dough should be shaggy, with visible chunks of butter. If needed, add 1 Tbsp more buttermilk. $\longrightarrow$

3   Transfer the dough to a lightly floured work surface and shape it into a disc. Wrap in plastic wrap and refrigerate for at least 1 hour or overnight. Refrigerated dough tightly wrapped in plastic wrap can be stored for up to 2 days. To make ahead, wrap the dough in plastic wrap and a layer of aluminum foil and freeze for up to 1 month. Then thaw in the fridge 1 day before you plan to bake.

4   Preheat the oven to 425°F [220°C].

5   On a lightly floured work surface, roll the dough into an 11 in [28 cm] circle and transfer to a 9 in [23 cm] pie plate. Trim the edges with kitchen scissors or a sharp knife, leaving a ½ in [13 mm] overhang around the edge. Tuck the excess dough under itself and crimp all around to seal the edges of the pie dough. Dock the bottom of the pie shell with a fork to prevent the dough from puffing up while it bakes. Chill the prepared pie crust in the refrigerator for 15 minutes prior to baking (this allows the gluten to relax, which prevents shrinking, and also lets the butter firm up, which gives us those flaky layers, so don't skip this step!).

6   Take a piece of parchment paper big enough to line the pie shell and crumple it up into a ball to make it more pliable. Smooth out the ball of parchment paper, fit it into the pie shell, and fill with uncooked rice, dried beans, or pie weights.

7   Bake for 15 to 20 minutes, until the edges start to set. Remove the crust from the oven and carefully lift the corners of the parchment paper to remove it along with the weights. In a small bowl, combine the beaten egg with 1 Tbsp of water and brush the bottom of the pie crust with a thin layer of this egg wash. Return the crust to the oven and bake for 2 to 3 more minutes, until the bottom is set and light golden brown in color. Let the crust cool completely on a wire rack.

8   **For the Filling:** Lower the oven temperature to 350°F [175°C].

9   Gently melt the chocolate and butter over a double boiler (see page 14). Once melted, remove from the heat, stir in the cocoa powder, and set aside to cool.

10   In a large bowl, whisk together the eggs and egg yolk. Add both sugars, the flour, and salt and whisk well until light, fluffy, and voluminous, 1 to 2 minutes. Add the buttermilk, vanilla, and espresso powder, if using, and whisk until incorporated. Pour in the chocolate mixture and whisk until well combined and no streaks remain.

11   Pour the filling into the cooled pie shell. Bake for 40 to 50 minutes, rotating halfway through. Cover the edges of the crust with foil if it browns too quickly. The edges of the filling should be set and the center should have a slight wobble. Let cool completely before serving. Top with whipped cream and chocolate shavings and serve. Store leftovers, covered, in the fridge for up to 3 days.

CHOCOLATE BANANA CREAM PIE

MAKES ONE 9 IN [23 CM] PIE	
PIE CRUST	
½ cup [115 g]	unsalted butter, cubed
¼ cup [60 g]	ice water, or more as needed
1¼ cups [156 g]	all-purpose flour
1 Tbsp	granulated sugar
¼ tsp	kosher salt
1	egg, beaten
CHOCOLATE BANANA PASTRY CREAM	
2	ripe bananas
2½ cups [600 g] plus 1 Tbsp	whole milk, plus more if needed, divided
1 Tbsp	vanilla bean paste or extract
4 oz [115 g]	60% dark chocolate, finely chopped
6	egg yolks
½ cup [100 g]	granulated sugar
2 Tbsp	light brown sugar, packed
¼ cup [32 g]	cornstarch, sifted
¾ tsp	kosher salt
ASSEMBLY	
½ cup [120 g]	heavy cream
2 Tbsp	granulated sugar
2 to 3	bananas, for pie crust
Whipped cream, for topping	
Chocolate shavings, for decoration	

The idea for this pie comes from pastry school, when we made banana-infused milk to serve with our chocolate chip cookies. I thought it was so ingenious at the time and always wanted to find a way to repurpose this idea. Then, a light bulb went off, and this banana cream pie was born—a banana-infused chocolate pastry cream sitting atop a layer of just-ripe bananas. Finally, a banana cream pie that lives up to its name with double the banana flavor. Fair warning: This is definitely a weekend baking project, so I recommend making the pie crust and pastry cream the day before to help break up the process. But trust me, it's definitely worth the effort!

DIRECTIONS

1 **For the Pie Crust:** Chill the butter and ice water separately in the freezer for 10 minutes to get extra cold.

2 In the bowl of a stand mixer fitted with the paddle attachment, add the flour, sugar, and salt and mix on low speed to combine. Add the butter and mix on low speed for 15 seconds until the pieces of butter are the size of walnut halves. With the mixer running on low speed, gradually pour in the ice water and mix for another 30 to 60 seconds, just until the dough starts to come together, taking care not to overmix. The dough should be shaggy, with visible chunks of butter. If needed, add 1 Tbsp more ice water. $\longrightarrow$

3 Transfer the dough to a lightly floured work surface and shape it into a disc. Wrap in plastic wrap and refrigerate for at least 1 hour or overnight. Refrigerated dough tightly wrapped in plastic wrap can be stored for up to 2 days. To make ahead, wrap the dough in plastic wrap and a layer of aluminum foil and freeze for up to 1 month. Then thaw in the fridge 1 day before you plan to bake.

4 **For the Chocolate Banana Pastry Cream:**
Slice the bananas into 2 in [5 cm] chunks and place them in a large heatproof bowl.

5 In a medium saucepan over medium heat, bring 2½ cups [600 g] of the milk to a boil, then pour it over the banana chunks. Add the vanilla and stir to combine. Let the banana milk cool, then cover the bowl with plastic wrap and refrigerate for at least 2 hours or overnight.

6 Place the chopped chocolate in a large mixing bowl and set aside.

7 Strain the banana milk, discarding the banana chunks, and measure the remaining milk in a glass measuring cup. You should have about 2 cups [480 g] remaining. If you're short, then top off with more milk until you have 2 cups [480 g]. Set aside.

8 In a large mixing bowl, combine the egg yolks, both sugars, cornstarch, the remaining 1 Tbsp of milk, and the salt.

9 In a large saucepan over medium heat, bring the banana milk just to a boil. Immediately remove from the heat and slowly stream the hot milk into the reserved egg mixture while whisking constantly to avoid curdling. This will temper the eggs.

10 Pour the tempered egg mixture back into the saucepan and cook over medium heat, whisking constantly. I like to start off with the whisk and then, once it starts to get thicker, I switch to a heatproof rubber spatula and make a figure-eight motion while stirring constantly. Bring the mixture to a boil and cook for 2 minutes, until the mixture is very thick or a digital thermometer reads 200°F [93°C].

11 To remove any cooked egg bits, strain the pastry cream through a fine-mesh sieve over the bowl of chopped chocolate. Whisk until the chocolate is melted and the pastry cream is smooth and emulsified. For an extra silky-smooth texture, use an immersion blender. Transfer the pastry cream to a shallow dish and set a piece of plastic wrap directly on the surface of the pastry cream to prevent a skin from forming. Let cool in the refrigerator for at least 4 hours or overnight.

12 **Blind Bake the Pie:** Preheat the oven to 425°F [220°C].

13 On a lightly floured work surface, roll the dough into an 11 in [28 cm] circle and transfer to a 9 in [23 cm] pie plate. Trim the edges with kitchen scissors or a sharp knife, leaving a ½ in [13 mm] overhang around the edge. Tuck the excess dough under itself and crimp all around to seal the edges of the pie dough. Dock the bottom of the pie shell with a fork to prevent the dough from puffing up while it bakes. Chill the prepared pie crust in the refrigerator for 15 minutes prior to baking (this allows the gluten to relax, which prevents shrinking, and also lets the butter firm up, which gives us those flaky layers, so don't skip this step!).

14 Take a piece of parchment paper big enough to line the pie shell and crumple it up into a ball to make it more pliable. Smooth out the ball of parchment paper, fit it into the pie shell, and fill with uncooked rice, dried beans, or pie weights.

15 Bake for 15 to 20 minutes, until the edges start to set. Remove the crust from the oven and carefully lift the corners of the parchment paper to remove it along with the weights. In a small bowl, combine the beaten egg with 1 Tbsp of water and brush the bottom of the pie crust with a thin layer of this egg wash. Return the crust to the oven and bake for 2 to 3 more minutes, until the bottom is set and light golden brown in color. Let the crust cool completely on a wire rack.

16 **To Assemble:** Using an electric hand mixer or a stand mixer fitted with the whisk attachment, whip the heavy cream and sugar just until soft peaks form. Fold in the chilled pastry cream and whip until combined and light and fluffy, taking care not to overwhip.

17 Spread a thin layer of the pastry cream into the bottom of the pie shell. Slice the bananas into ¼ in [6 mm] thick round coins and arrange the slices in an even layer over the bottom of the pie shell.

18 Scoop the remaining pastry cream over the banana slices and smooth the top with an offset spatula. Cover and refrigerate for 4 hours to set.

19 When ready to serve, top with more whipped cream and chocolate shavings for decoration. Store any leftovers, covered, in the refrigerator for up to 3 days.

MORNING TREATS

N° 7

RISE / SHINE

CHOCOLATE LOVER

LEMON-RASPBERRY WHITE CHOCOLATE MUFFINS

MAKES 12 TO 15 MUFFINS	
1 cup [200 g]	granulated sugar, plus more for sprinkling
1 Tbsp	lemon zest
2 cups [250 g]	all-purpose flour
2½ tsp	baking powder
½ tsp	kosher salt
½ cup [120 g]	buttermilk, well shaken, at room temperature
¼ cup [60 g]	sour cream, at room temperature
1 Tbsp	lemon juice
1 tsp	vanilla extract
6 oz [170 g]	fresh raspberries
½ cup [115 g]	unsalted butter, at room temperature
2	eggs, at room temperature
1 cup [170 g]	white chocolate chips

Brimming with juicy raspberries, zesty lemon, and smooth white chocolate, these muffins are the complete package. For muffins that rival the bakeries', there are a few tips I follow. First, I gently fold in the dry ingredients without overmixing to create a delicate, tender crumb. Second, I let the muffin batter rest to help develop the flavor and moisture. It also makes for a wonderful make-ahead solution for those busy (or slow!) mornings. Lastly, I start baking the muffins at a high temperature then lower the temperature in order to get a domed muffin top.

DIRECTIONS

1 In a small bowl, rub together the sugar and lemon zest to release the oils from the zest. Set aside.

2 In a medium bowl, whisk together the flour, baking powder, and salt. Set aside.

3 In another medium bowl, whisk together the buttermilk, sour cream, lemon juice, and vanilla. Set aside.

4 If your raspberries are big, cut them into smaller pieces closer to the size of a blueberry, being careful not to bruise or mash the berries. Remove 1 Tbsp of the flour mixture and toss the berries to coat. (This will help prevent them from sinking and will also absorb some of the excess moisture.) →

5 In the bowl of a stand mixer fitted with the paddle attachment, beat together the butter and sugar mixture for 5 minutes, until light and fluffy. Add the eggs one at a time, mixing well after each addition. Add half of the flour mixture and mix on low speed until incorporated. Pour in the buttermilk mixture and mix on low speed until combined, scraping down the bowl as necessary. Add the remaining flour and mix for another 30 seconds, until no streaks remain. Gently fold in the white chocolate chips and raspberries just until incorporated. Let the batter rest for 15 minutes, or cover and let rest overnight in the fridge if you want to make ahead.

6 Preheat the oven to 425°F [220°C]. Line a standard muffin tin with paper liners.

7 Scoop the batter into each cup using an ice cream scoop, about three-quarters full. Sprinkle the top of each muffin with sugar. Bake for 5 minutes, then lower the heat to 350°F [175°C] and bake for another 15 to 20 minutes or until a toothpick inserted into the center of a muffin comes out clean. Transfer to a wire rack to let cool. Store, covered, at room temperature for up to 4 days.

VARIATIONS

Double Chocolate Chip Muffins: Omit the lemon zest, lemon juice, and raspberries. Substitute the flour with 1½ cups [190 g] all-purpose flour and ½ cup [45 g] Dutch-process cocoa powder. Increase the sour cream to ⅔ cup [160 g] and substitute the white chocolate chips with semisweet chocolate chips. Bake at 425°F [220°C] for 5 minutes and then at 350°F [175°C] for 12 to 15 minutes.

Chocolate Chip Muffins: Omit the lemon zest, lemon juice, and raspberries. Increase the sour cream to ½ cup [120 g] and substitute the white chocolate with mini semisweet chocolate chips. Bake at 425°F [220°C] for 5 minutes and then at 350°F [175°C] for 12 to 15 minutes.

CHOCOLATE CHIP STREUSEL COFFEE CAKE

MAKES ONE 8 IN [20 CM] CAKE	
COCOA STREUSEL	
½ cup [65 g]	all-purpose flour
½ cup [100 g]	light brown sugar, packed
1 Tbsp	Dutch-process cocoa powder
1 tsp	ground cinnamon
¼ tsp	kosher salt
¼ cup [57 g]	unsalted butter, cubed
COCOA CINNAMON SUGAR FILLING	
¼ cup [50 g]	light brown sugar, packed
2 Tbsp	all-purpose flour
2 tsp	Dutch-process cocoa powder
2 tsp	ground cinnamon
CHOCOLATE CHIP COFFEE CAKE	
1½ cups [190 g]	all-purpose flour
¾ tsp	baking powder
¾ tsp	baking soda
½ tsp	kosher salt
½ cup [115 g]	unsalted butter, at room temperature
¾ cup [150 g]	granulated sugar
2	large eggs, at room temperature
¾ cup [180 g]	sour cream, at room temperature
¼ cup [60 g]	buttermilk, well shaken, or whole milk, at room temperature
1 tsp	vanilla extract
½ cup [85 g]	mini semisweet chocolate chips

Coffee cake is hands down my favorite breakfast treat. This recipe is a nod to the boxed version I grew up on and have fond memories of. Every Saturday, as soon as I would roll out of bed, I would be greeted with a leftover slice of coffee cake that my dad had made hours before. I've since graduated from the boxed mix and have moved onto this chocolate chip coffee cake. The buttery streusel is a prerequisite for any proper coffee cake; I add cocoa powder for an extra dose of chocolate. For an extra-thick streusel topping, don't be shy and double the recipe.

DIRECTIONS

1 **For the Cocoa Streusel:** In a medium bowl, whisk together the flour, sugar, cocoa powder, cinnamon, and salt. Add the butter and use your fingers to work it into the flour mixture by rubbing it between your fingertips, pressing and pinching the butter into the dry ingredients. Continue until the butter is evenly distributed and the mixture resembles coarse crumbs with some pea-size pieces of butter. Set aside.

2 **For the Cocoa Cinnamon Sugar Filling:** In a small bowl, whisk together the sugar, flour, cocoa powder, and cinnamon. Set aside. →

3 **For the Chocolate Chip Coffee Cake:**
Preheat the oven to 350°F [175°C]. Line an 8 in [20 cm] square baking pan with parchment paper and grease with nonstick spray.

4 In a medium bowl, whisk together the flour, baking powder, baking soda, and salt.

5 In the bowl of a stand mixer fitted with the paddle attachment, beat together the butter and sugar for 5 minutes, until light and fluffy. Add the eggs one at a time, mixing well after each addition. Add the sour cream, buttermilk, and vanilla and mix on low speed just until incorporated. Fold in the flour mixture, then the chocolate chips just until combined.

6 Pour the batter into the prepared pan and smooth the top with an offset spatula. Sprinkle the top with the streusel. Bake for 35 to 45 minutes or until a toothpick inserted comes out with a few moist crumbs. Transfer to a wire rack to cool completely. Slice and serve with a cup of hot coffee. Store, covered, at room temperature for up to 3 days.

CHOCOLATE CHIP BANANA NUT SCONES

MAKES 6 SCONES	
10 Tbsp [140 g]	cold unsalted butter
2½ cups [315 g]	all-purpose flour
⅓ cup [67 g]	light brown sugar, packed
2 Tbsp	granulated sugar
2 tsp	baking powder
½ tsp	baking soda
½ tsp	kosher salt
½ cup [120 g]	mashed banana (about 1 large banana)
1	egg, plus 1 egg lightly beaten, for the egg wash
⅓ cup [80 g]	heavy cream, plus more as needed
1 tsp	vanilla extract
¾ cup [130 g]	semisweet chocolate chips
¼ cup [35 g]	coarsely chopped toasted walnuts
Turbinado sugar, for sprinkling	

If you love banana bread, you'll fall head over heels for these chocolate chip banana nut scones. There's a lot of debate about whether grating your butter or cutting in cold cubes into the flour is better for scones. I prefer to grate the butter because it's easy to mix in, it disperses evenly throughout the flour, and because that's how Grandma does it. Who am I to disagree? To get flaky layers, I make a "shortcut" lamination by rolling out the dough, cutting it into thirds, stacking the thirds, and then rolling it out. It's a cheat, but it works every time.

DIRECTIONS

1   Using a box grater, shred the cold butter onto a piece of parchment paper. Slide the parchment paper onto a plate and freeze for 10 minutes to chill.

2   In a large bowl, combine the flour, both sugars, baking powder, baking soda, and salt. Set aside.

3   In a large glass measuring cup, combine the banana with the beaten egg, heavy cream, and vanilla with a fork until homogeneous. Set aside.

4   Add the chilled butter to the flour mixture and toss until incorporated. Slowly add in the banana mixture and combine using a rubber spatula. Mix just until combined, working fast and taking care not to overwork the dough. Add the chocolate chips and walnuts and fold until incorporated. At this point, the dough should look shaggy; it shouldn't be a wet, fully combined dough like cookie dough. If it's too dry, add 1 Tbsp of heavy cream.   →

5   Transfer the dough onto a lightly floured surface and pat into a 12 in [30 cm] long rectangle, collecting any dry bits or excess flour using a bench scraper. Cut the dough in half into two 6 in [15 cm] pieces and stack them, pressing any loose flour or dry bits in between the layers. If there are any exposed wet bits, dust with extra flour. Roll the dough into a 12 in [30 cm] long rectangle again and cut in half once more and stack. If there are still any remaining dry bits or loose flour, press those crumbs into the layers. Roll the dough into a 1 in [2.5 cm] thick rectangle about 12 by 4 in [30 by 10 cm], shaping the edges with a bench scraper. Transfer the dough onto a parchment paper–lined baking sheet and chill in the freezer for 10 minutes to firm up.

6   Preheat the oven to 400°F [200°C].

7   Divide the dough into six triangles and arrange on a parchment paper–lined baking sheet, leaving space between each scone. Lightly beat the remaining egg with 1 Tbsp of water to make an egg wash. Brush the top of each scone with the egg wash and sprinkle with turbinado sugar. Chill in the freezer for another 10 minutes for good measure.

8   Bake for 15 to 20 minutes, or until golden brown. Transfer to a wire rack to cool slightly, and serve warm. Scones are best eaten fresh the day they are made.

VARIATION

Pumpkin Chocolate Chip Scones: Substitute the mashed banana with ½ cup [120 g] pumpkin purée, patted dry.

CHOCOLATE FRANGIPANE CROISSANTS

MAKES 8 CROISSANTS	
1 cup plus 1 Tbsp [115 g]	blanched almond flour
2 Tbsp	all-purpose flour
2 Tbsp	Dutch-process cocoa powder
½ tsp	kosher salt
½ tsp	ground cardamom (optional)
½ cup [115 g]	unsalted butter, at room temperature
½ cup [100 g]	granulated sugar
2	eggs, at room temperature
3 oz [85 g]	dark chocolate, melted and cooled
1 tsp	vanilla extract
8	store-bought croissants
Sliced almonds, for sprinkling	
Confectioners' sugar, for dusting	

At the bakery I once worked at, one of my earliest tasks was making frangipane and piping it into hundreds and hundreds of croissants every day. They were among our best sellers and always sold out. I often find myself missing those delightful pastries, so I've developed an easy, at-home chocolate version that's just as delicious. By making your own almond cream (the secret is toasted almond flour), you can add a touch of elegance and transform ordinary, store-bought croissants into a sophisticated treat just like they do at the bakeries. Quick and easy to make, they're perfect for parties, and your guests will be none the wiser, thinking you've spent hours in the kitchen creating these fancy delights. Enjoy the accolades and these effortless yet impressive pastries.

DIRECTIONS

1   Preheat the oven to 350°F [175°C]. Line a baking sheet with parchment paper.

2   In a medium skillet over medium heat, toast the almond flour, stirring frequently, until golden brown, 5 to 8 minutes. Remove from the heat and set aside to cool.

3   In a medium bowl, whisk together the almond flour, all-purpose flour, cocoa powder, salt, and cardamom, if using.

4   In a large mixing bowl using a hand mixer, beat together the butter and sugar until light and fluffy, about 2 minutes. Add the eggs one at a time, incorporating completely, before adding the next one. Add the flour mixture and beat just until combined. Fold in the melted chocolate and vanilla, mixing until incorporated.   →

5 Slice the croissants in half lengthwise. Using a pastry bag fitted with a ½ in [13 mm] round tip, pipe the bottom half with frangipane in a zigzag motion. Place the top half over the bottom and then pipe a small dollop of frangipane on top. Press sliced almonds into the frangipane.

6 Arrange the croissants on the baking sheet, evenly spaced. Bake for 20 to 25 minutes, until the almonds are golden and the frangipane is set. Dust the tops with confectioners' sugar. Serve warm or at room temperature. They are best enjoyed the day they are made.

VARIATION

Hazelnut Frangipane: Substitute the almond flour with an equal amount of hazelnut flour.

CRISPY CHOCOLATE BUTTERMILK WAFFLES

MAKES 8 BELGIAN WAFFLES	
2 cups [480 g]	buttermilk, well shaken
¾ cup [170 g]	unsalted butter, melted and cooled
2	large eggs, separated
1 tsp	vanilla extract
1½ cups [190 g]	all-purpose flour
½ cup [65 g]	cornstarch, sifted
¼ cup [20 g]	Dutch-process cocoa powder
5 Tbsp [60 g]	granulated sugar
1 tsp	baking powder
1 tsp	baking soda
1 tsp	kosher salt
½ cup [85 g]	mini semisweet chocolate chips
Butter or maple syrup (optional), for topping	
Confectioners' sugar (optional), for dusting	

Whenever I slept over at my grandparents' house, I would always wake up to the aroma of homemade waffles. The smell of the batter cooking and the beeping of the waffle iron was enough motivation to get me out of bed. My grandma made the best waffles fresh to order—always incredibly crispy, light, and airy and dusted with a sprinkling of confectioners' sugar. They were exactly what a waffle should be. I have fond memories of watching her stand at the counter as I patiently waited for my plate. I still have her handwritten recipe, and I've since adapted it into a decadent double chocolate waffle. The secret is cornstarch and whipped egg whites. Subbing some of the flour for cornstarch creates a crispy exterior, and folding whipped egg whites into the batter creates an airy batter and texture.

DIRECTIONS

1 In a medium bowl, beat together the buttermilk, melted butter, egg yolks, and vanilla.

2 In a large bowl, whisk together the flour, cornstarch, cocoa powder, sugar, baking powder, baking soda, and salt. Pour the wet ingredients into the flour mixture and mix just until combined; a few small lumps may remain.

3 In a medium bowl using a hand mixer or whisk, whip the egg whites until soft peaks form. Gently fold the whites into the batter, being careful not to deflate them. Fold in the chocolate chips. Let the batter rest for 15 minutes.

4 Preheat your waffle iron and grease with nonstick spray. Pour a portion of batter into the waffle iron and cook according to the manufacturer's directions, until crispy and cooked through. Repeat with the remaining batter.

5 Transfer the waffles to a wire rack so they don't steam and get soggy. Serve immediately with butter, syrup, and a dusting of confectioners' sugar, if desired, just like at Grandma's. Waffles are best eaten hot and fresh while they're still crispy, but leftovers can be stored in a gallon freezer-safe bag in the freezer for up to 1 month; toast the waffles to reheat.

FRIED AND CHILLED

CHOCOLATE LOVER

NEAPOLITAN ICEBOX CAKE

MAKES 8 SERVINGS	
¾ cup [12 g]	freeze-dried strawberries
2 cups [480 g]	heavy cream
8 oz [225 g]	mascarpone
¾ cup [90 g]	confectioners' sugar, sifted
1 tsp	vanilla extract
¼ tsp	kosher salt
2 Tbsp	Dutch-process cocoa powder
25	chocolate wafer cookies, or Oreo cookie halves with filling removed

There's a reason classics never go out of style, and icebox cakes are a prime example. I love icebox cakes for their nostalgia and sheer simplicity. All you need is a few ingredients and some time—the hardest part is waiting for it to chill. Easily adaptable into any flavor your heart desires, my go-to favorite is the beloved Neapolitan. Layers of chocolate wafers sandwiched between soft, billowy mounds of chocolate, vanilla, and strawberry whipped cream makes for a winning combination and visually stunning treat. Grinding freeze-dried strawberries into a powder adds a vibrant pop of color and concentrated flavor boost without compromising the texture.

DIRECTIONS

1 In a spice grinder or food processor, grind the freeze-dried strawberries into a powder. Set aside.

2 In the bowl of a stand mixer fitted with the whisk attachment, combine the heavy cream, mascarpone, sugar, vanilla, and salt. Start mixing on low speed until incorporated, then increase the speed to medium and mix until you have stiff peaks.

3 Divide the cream into thirds, leaving one third in the stand mixer and transferring the other two into separate mixing bowls. In one of the mixing bowls, sift in the cocoa powder and gently fold with a rubber spatula, taking care not to deflate the cream. Sift the strawberry powder over the other bowl and gently fold with a rubber spatula. Set aside.

4 Lightly grease a 9 by 5 in [23 by 13 cm] loaf pan and line with plastic wrap, leaving an overhang on two sides. →

5   To assemble, spoon half of the strawberry cream into the bottom of the loaf pan and spread evenly using the back of a spoon or rubber spatula. Place a single layer of 10 cookies (5 rows by 2 columns) on top of the strawberry cream. Layer half of the vanilla whipped cream and another layer of cookies. Add a layer of half of the chocolate whipped cream followed by a layer of cookies. Repeat in the same order with the remaining creams (strawberry, vanilla, chocolate) finishing the top layer with the chocolate cream. There should be a total of 6 layers of cream and 5 layers of cookies. Bring the excess plastic wrap from the sides of the loaf pan over the top and gently cover the surface of the chocolate cream. Transfer to the refrigerator and chill for at least 8 hours or overnight to soften the cookies.

6   To serve, unwrap the plastic wrap from the top of the cake, invert onto a cutting board, and carefully peel away the remaining plastic wrap from the sides. Cut into slices using a sharp knife dipped in hot water and wiped dry between each slice. Store any leftovers tightly wrapped in the refrigerator for up to 2 days.

CHOCOLATE OLD FASHIONED DOUGHNUTS

MAKES 9 DOUGHNUTS	
CHOCOLATE OLD FASHIONED DOUGHNUTS	
2 cups [250 g]	cake flour, plus more for dusting
½ cup [45 g]	Dutch-process cocoa powder
1½ tsp	baking powder
1 tsp	kosher salt
½ tsp	ground nutmeg
½ cup [120 g]	sour cream
¼ cup [60 g]	buttermilk, well shaken
½ cup [100 g]	granulated sugar
2 Tbsp	unsalted butter, at room temperature
2	large egg yolks
½ tsp	vanilla extract
Neutral oil, for frying	
GLAZE	
¼ cup [60 g]	whole milk
2 Tbsp	unsalted butter, cubed
2 cups [240 g]	confectioners' sugar, sifted
1 tsp	light corn syrup
½ tsp	vanilla extract

NOTE ○ If you don't have buttermilk, replace it with ¼ cup [60 g] sour cream (for a total of ¾ cup [180 g] sour cream).

I can confidently say that old fashioned doughnuts are the superior doughnut. You can't beat the crispy, craggy exterior and cakey center. Thankfully, they're incredibly easy to make at home and don't require yeast, so there's no need to worry about proofing. The hardest part is rolling out the dough. For this recipe, I like to make the dough the day before, refrigerate overnight, and then wake up and fry up a fresh batch of doughnuts with a strong coffee in hand. The secret to the light texture is the cake flour, which has a lower protein content than all-purpose. And the key to achieving those crispy edges is to fry both sides twice. Use a Dutch oven and a candy thermometer to ensure even heat distribution and better temperature control.

DIRECTIONS

1 **For the Chocolate Old Fashioned Doughnuts:** In a medium bowl, whisk together the flour, cocoa powder, baking powder, salt, and nutmeg. Set aside.

2 In a small bowl, combine the sour cream and buttermilk.

3 In a stand mixer fitted with the paddle attachment, beat the sugar and butter on low speed for 1 minute. Add the egg yolks and vanilla, then mix on medium speed for 1 minute until combined. Add the dry mixture in three separate additions, alternating with the sour cream mixture (dry, wet, dry, wet, dry). Mix each addition on low speed just until combined, making sure to scrape down the bowl between each addition. →

4   Wrap the dough in plastic wrap and shape into a 4 by 6 in [10 by 15 cm] rectangle. Refrigerate for at least 4 hours or overnight.

5   Line a baking sheet with parchment paper. Line another baking sheet with paper towels and place a wire rack on top.

6   Transfer the dough to a generously floured work surface. Roll the dough to a ½ in [13 mm] thickness and cut out rounds using a 3 in [7.5 cm] cutter, then cut out holes in the rounds using a 1 in [2.5 cm] round cutter. Dip the cutters into flour between each cut to prevent sticking. Gently re-roll the scraps and repeat the process.

7   Transfer the doughnuts to the parchment paper–lined baking sheet. Optionally, to encourage more craggy edges, use a razor blade or sharp knife to score a square around the top of the doughnut, making sure not to cut all the way through. Keep the doughnuts in the refrigerator until the oil is ready.

8   In a large Dutch oven over medium heat, heat 2 in [5 cm] of oil until a thermometer registers 325°F [160°C].

9   Working in batches, gently transfer the doughnuts to the oil. Once they start to float, after 10 to 15 seconds, flip and fry for 90 seconds. Flip again and fry for another 90 seconds. Then flip again and fry for 60 seconds. Flip and fry for a final 60 seconds. Transfer the doughnuts to the prepared wire rack to drain.

10 **For the Glaze:** In a medium saucepan over low heat, combine the milk and butter until the butter is completely melted. Add the confectioners' sugar and whisk until smooth. Stir in the corn syrup and vanilla and heat until well combined.

11 Dip the tops of the doughnuts into the warm glaze and let them drip right-side up on the wire rack. Let the glaze set for 10 to 15 minutes before serving. Store in an airtight container at room temperature for up to 3 days.

RICOTTA CHOUX CRULLERS

MAKES 9 CRULLERS	
RICOTTA PÂTE À CHOUX	
¼ cup [57 g]	unsalted butter, cubed
¾ cup [180 g]	water
1 Tbsp	granulated sugar
1 tsp	vanilla extract
½ tsp	kosher salt
1¼ cups [156 g]	all-purpose flour, sifted
4	large eggs
½ cup [120 g]	whole-milk ricotta, well drained
Neutral oil, for frying	
CHOCOLATE GLAZE	
¼ cup [60 g]	whole milk
2 Tbsp	unsalted butter, cubed
1¾ cups [210 g]	confectioners' sugar, sifted
¼ cup [20 g]	Dutch-process cocoa powder, sifted
1 tsp	light corn syrup
½ tsp	vanilla extract
Sprinkles or mini chocolate chips, for topping	

Pâte à choux, a versatile pastry dough made from simple ingredients, can truly do it all. It's an overachiever. The same basic dough can be used to make éclairs, cream puffs, gougères, churros, or crullers. But I'd say crullers might be my favorite application. They have a thin, crispy exterior and a light, custardy inside that is delightfully eggy. To make these extra special, I decided to add a bit of ricotta to the dough and then dip them in a dark chocolate ganache that hugs all its swirled ridges. And, as always with fried food, I recommend eating it as fresh as possible.

DIRECTIONS

1 **For the Ricotta Pâte à Choux:** Cut nine 3 in [7.5 cm] squares of parchment paper and evenly space them out on a baking sheet. (These will be used to hold the proofed crullers, making it easier to transfer to the hot oil without deflating them.)

2 In a medium saucepan over medium heat, combine the water, butter, sugar, vanilla, and salt and bring to a rolling boil. Immediately remove from the heat and add the flour all at once.

3 Whisk until there are no lumps. Gently shake the dough off the whisk and then switch to a rubber spatula. →

4   Return the saucepan to medium heat and cook for 2 minutes, stirring constantly with the spatula. You know the dough is ready when you see a thin skin form on the bottom of the pot and the dough has formed into a ball. This ensures you have evaporated some of the moisture.

5   Transfer the dough to the bowl of a stand mixer fitted with the paddle attachment. Mix on low speed until the dough cools down to 140°F [60°C] or until the steam dissipates (this ensures you won't cook the eggs).

6   With the mixer running on low speed, add the eggs one at a time, scraping down the bowl and ensuring each one is fully incorporated before adding the next. The dough will look curdled, but rest assured it will come together within a few seconds. Add the ricotta and mix until combined. Finish by mixing on medium speed for 30 seconds to make sure everything is incorporated. The final consistency should be pipeable and not too stiff.

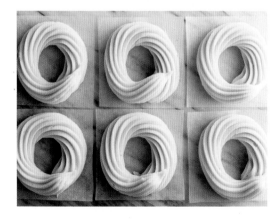

7   Transfer the dough to a pastry bag fitted with a ½ in [13 mm] star tip (I recommend Ateco #829 star tip). Pipe the crullers onto the prepared parchment paper pieces in a circle shape while applying even pressure. Overlap the ends by gently releasing pressure on the pastry bag and pulling up at the end. Wet your finger with water and gently seal the ends.

8   Place a wire rack on a baking sheet lined with paper towels and set aside. In a large heavy-bottom pot, pour in about 2 in [5 cm] of oil and heat over medium heat until a thermometer registers 350°F [175°C].

9   Working in batches, gently transfer the crullers to the oil with the parchment paper still attached. Cook for 3 minutes on each side, discarding the parchment paper after flipping. Transfer the crullers to the prepared wire rack to drain.

10   **For the Chocolate Glaze:** In a medium saucepan over low heat, combine the milk and butter until the butter is completely melted. Add the confectioners' sugar and cocoa powder and whisk until smooth. Stir in the corn syrup and vanilla and heat until well combined.

11   Dip the tops of the crullers into the warm glaze and let them drip right-side up on the wire rack. Top with sprinkles or mini chocolate chips for decoration. Crullers are best served immediately.

CHOCOLATE MASCARPONE CUSTARD DOUGHNUTS

MAKES 15 DOUGHNUTS	
BRIOCHE DOUGHNUTS	
3¼ cups [405 g]	bread flour
¾ cups [95 g]	all-purpose flour
⅓ cup [67 g]	granulated sugar
2¼ tsp	instant yeast
1½ tsp	kosher salt
1 cup [240 g]	whole milk, warmed to 110°F [45°C]
2	eggs
1	egg yolk
1½ tsp	vanilla extract
½ cup [115 g]	unsalted butter, cubed, at room temperature
Neutral oil, for frying	
CHOCOLATE MASCARPONE CUSTARD	
4 oz [115 g]	60% dark chocolate, finely chopped
6	egg yolks
½ cup plus 2 Tbsp [125 g]	granulated sugar, divided
¼ cup [32 g]	cornstarch
1 Tbsp	cocoa powder
2 cups [480 g]	whole milk, divided
½ tsp	kosher salt
1 tsp	vanilla extract
½ cup [120 g]	mascarpone
CACAO NIB SUGAR COATING	
1½ cups [300 g]	granulated sugar
3 Tbsp	cacao nibs, finely ground

If you find yourself with a little time on your hands and are looking for a weekend project, then bring the doughnut shop home and add these to your priority list, because there's nothing quite like a freshly fried doughnut. These yeast-raised treats use a mix of bread flour and all-purpose flour, which produces a tender and pillowy dough. The custard has a deep chocolate flavor from both cocoa powder and melted chocolate and is whipped to perfection with mascarpone for a subtle tang. And, to round it off, the doughnuts are rolled in a cacao nib sugar to add a toasty aroma and flavor. So turn the hot-and-fresh sign on and enjoy the fruits of your labor.

DIRECTIONS

1 **For the Brioche Doughnuts:** Place both flours, the sugar, yeast, and salt in the bowl of a stand mixer; do not mix. Pour in the warm milk, then add the eggs, egg yolk, and vanilla. Fit the stand mixer with the dough hook attachment and mix on low speed until incorporated, then increase the speed to medium. Knead for 10 to 15 minutes, until the dough starts to pull away from the sides of the bowl and develops elasticity.

2 Scrape down the bowl to ensure any dry bits are incorporated. With the mixer running on low speed, add the butter pieces one at a time, waiting until each piece is incorporated. Be patient and do not add it all at once or you may break the gluten structure. If needed, stop to scrape down the bowl to make sure all the butter is incorporated. →

3 Once the butter is fully incorporated, mix again on medium speed for another 10 minutes, or until the dough is smooth, elastic like a rubber band, and clears the sides of the bowl.

4 Lightly grease a bowl or quart container with nonstick spray and transfer the dough. Cover the bowl with plastic wrap or a clean dish towel and let the dough rise for 1 hour at room temperature or until it has doubled in size.

5 Once the dough has doubled in size, punch the dough to degas it, then cover it with plastic wrap and transfer to the refrigerator to chill overnight.

6 **For the Chocolate Mascarpone Custard:** Place the chopped chocolate in a large bowl and set aside.

7 In another large bowl, add the egg yolks, ¼ cup [50 g] of the sugar, the cornstarch, and cocoa powder and whisk to combine. Add a few Tbsp of the milk to thin it out and whisk to combine.

8 In a medium saucepan over medium heat, bring the remaining milk, the remaining ¼ cup [50 g] plus 2 Tbsp of sugar, and the salt to a boil. Remove from the heat and slowly stream the hot milk into the egg mixture while whisking constantly; this will temper the eggs. Pour the tempered egg mixture back into the saucepan and cook over medium heat, whisking constantly, until the mixture starts to thicken and boil, at least 1 minute to cook off any raw cornstarch flavor.

9 Pass the mixture through a fine-mesh sieve over the chopped chocolate and stir until the chocolate is melted. Add the vanilla and whisk until homogenous. For a silky-smooth texture, use an immersion blender to emulsify.

10 Transfer to a container and place plastic wrap directly onto the surface of the custard to prevent a skin from forming. Let cool in the refrigerator for at least 4 hours or overnight.

11 **For the Cacao Nib Sugar Coating:** In a small, airtight container, combine the sugar and ground cacao nibs. Reserve until ready to use.

12 **To Assemble:** Cut fifteen 3 in [7.5 cm] squares out of parchment paper and evenly space them out on a baking sheet. (These will be used to hold the proofed doughnuts, making it easier to transfer to the hot oil without deflating them.) Set a wire rack on top of a paper towel–lined baking sheet.

13 Transfer the cacao nib sugar into a shallow bowl or pan, ready for coating the doughnuts.

14 Transfer the dough to a lightly floured work surface and divide into 15 portions (about 2¼ oz [65 g] each). Flatten a portion with the heel of your hand, bring the corners to the middle, roll into a ball, and shape into a tight bun with the cup of your hand. Place on a parchment square and repeat with the remaining dough. Cover loosely with plastic wrap and let proof at room temperature for about 1 hour or until doubled in size. →

15 About 20 minutes before you're ready to fry, fill a Dutch oven halfway with oil. Attach a candy thermometer to the side of the Dutch oven and set over medium-high heat until the oil reaches 350°F [175°C].

16 Working in batches so as not to overcrowd the pot, gently drop the doughnuts into the oil with the parchment paper attached, taking care not to deflate the doughnuts. Carefully remove parchment paper with metal tongs, as it should be easy to release after a few seconds.

17 Fry for 2 minutes on each side, until golden brown. If the doughnuts bob around in the oil, you may need to use a metal spider to gently push them down to encourage even browning. Transfer the doughnuts to the prepared wire rack. While still hot but cool enough to handle, roll the doughnuts in the cacao nib sugar and then place back on the rack.

18 Repeat with remaining doughnuts, while keeping an eye on the temperature of the oil. It's important to make sure the oil is at temperature before frying a new batch.

19 Allow doughnuts to cool completely before filling. When ready to fill the doughnuts, add the mascarpone to the chilled custard and whip with a hand mixer until light and silky smooth. Fill a pastry bag fitted with a round pastry tip. Use the tip to pierce a hole in the side of a doughnut between the grease line, and pipe the custard into the doughnut until it puffs up and you can feel the doughnut getting heavier. Repeat the process with the remaining doughnuts. Doughnuts are best eaten the day they are made, but leftovers can be stored in an airtight container in the fridge for up to 2 days.

CHOCOLATE HAZELNUT SEMIFREDDO

MAKES 8 SERVINGS	
CHOCOLATE SEMIFREDDO	
⅓ cup [45 g]	hazelnuts
4 oz [115 g]	70% bittersweet chocolate, chopped
5	egg yolks
¾ cup [150 g]	granulated sugar
3 Tbsp	Dutch-process cocoa powder
½ tsp	kosher salt
1¼ cups [300 g]	heavy cream
½ cup [120 g]	mascarpone
1 Tbsp	Frangelico (optional)
NUTELLA SAUCE	
4 tsp	whole milk
¼ cup [65 g]	Nutella

When the annual summer heat wave hits here in Southern California, my craving for something cold and sweet increases while my motivation to do anything decreases. I love semifreddo because it can satisfy my ice cream craving without the hassle and time commitment of using an ice cream maker. This Italian dessert's name translates to "half-cold," referring to its luscious, frozen, mousse-like texture that's lighter than ice cream and just melts on your tongue. The key is whipping egg yolks and sugar together, known as a pate à bombe, then gently folding in cream and mascarpone to create a mixture that remains soft, airy, and creamy when frozen. With the addition of toasted hazelnuts for a bit of crunch, a splash of Frangelico for an extra kick, and a warm drizzle of Nutella on top, this is the perfect indulgence on a hot summer day!

DIRECTIONS

1 **For the Chocolate Semifreddo:** Preheat the oven to 325°F [160°C]. Lightly grease a 9 by 5 in [23 by 13 cm] loaf pan and line with plastic wrap, leaving an overhang on two sides.

2 Toast the hazelnuts in the oven for 10 to 15 minutes, until fragrant. Remove the skins as best as you can, then roughly chop into small pieces. Set aside.

3 Gently melt the chocolate over a double boiler (see page 14). Cool to room temperature.

4 In the bowl of a stand mixer fitted with the whisk attachment, whip the egg yolks on medium-high speed for 5 minutes, until light and frothy and doubled in volume.

5 While the egg yolks are whipping, in a small saucepan, combine the sugar and ¼ cup [60 ml] of water. Use your finger to incorporate the sugar and water until the mixture resembles wet sand. Wet your hand and clean the sides of the saucepan to remove any remaining dry bits of sugar. Cook the sugar syrup over high heat until it reaches 240°F [115°C]; immediately remove from the heat. →

6   With the mixer running on medium speed, pour the hot sugar syrup down the sides of the bowl, being careful to avoid hitting the whisk attachment, otherwise the sugar droplets will solidify. Once the sugar syrup is fully incorporated, increase the speed to high and whip for another 5 minutes, until the mixture has cooled. Add the melted chocolate, cocoa powder, and salt to the egg mixture and whisk to combine.

7   In a separate bowl, whip the heavy cream, mascarpone, and Frangelico, if using, until soft peaks form. Fold into the cooled egg mixture in three separate additions until fully combined, adding the chopped hazelnuts in the last addition.

8   Pour the chocolate semifreddo mixture into the prepared loaf pan and spread evenly with an offset spatula. Place plastic wrap directly on the surface and chill in the freezer for at least 8 hours or ideally overnight.

9   When ready to serve, lift the semifreddo from the pan using the plastic wrap as handles and transfer to a serving plate. Let stand for 5 minutes to take off the chill. In the meantime, make the Nutella sauce.

10 **For the Nutella Sauce:** Microwave the milk in a small bowl for 30 seconds, just until hot. Add the Nutella and mix until combined.

11 Cut the semifreddo into slices, using a sharp knife dipped in hot water and wiped dry between each slice. Serve with a drizzle of warm Nutella sauce. Keep leftovers tightly wrapped in the freezer for up to 1 month.

VARIATION

Rocky Road Semifreddo: Add 1 cup [57 g] of mini marshmallows for a rocky road twist!

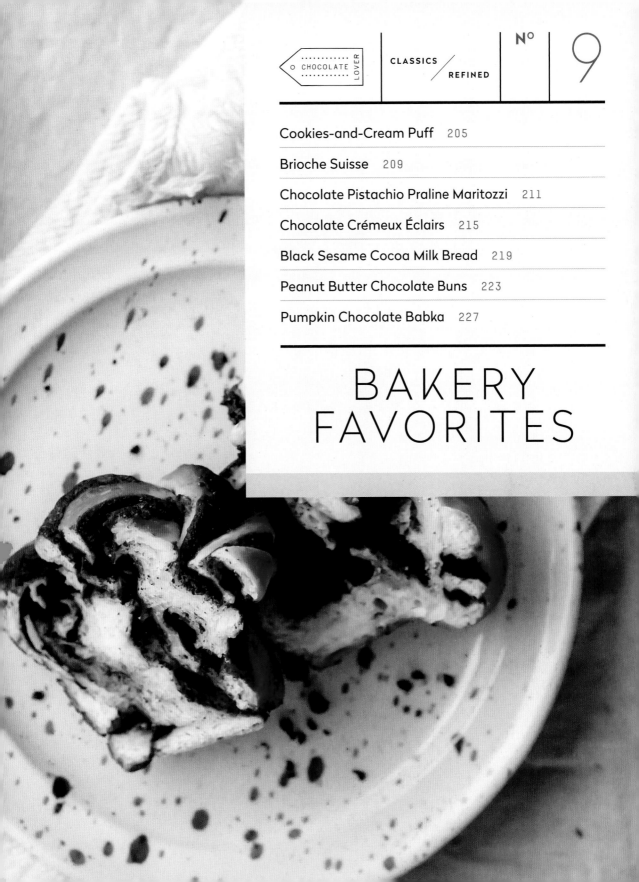

BAKERY FAVORITES

COOKIES-AND-CREAM PUFF

MAKES 16 CREAM PUFFS	
WHITE CHOCOLATE NAMELAKA	
1½ tsp	powdered gelatin, such as Knox
10 oz [285 g]	white chocolate, finely chopped
⅔ cup [160 g]	whole milk
1 Tbsp	vanilla bean paste or extract
½ tsp	kosher salt
¾ cup [180 g]	heavy cream
½ cup [120 g]	mascarpone
10	Oreo cookies, with filling removed
CHOCOLATE CRAQUELIN COOKIE	
6 Tbsp [85 g]	unsalted butter, at room temperature
⅓ cup plus 1 Tbsp [80 g]	light brown sugar, packed
⅛ tsp	kosher salt
⅔ cup [85 g]	all-purpose flour
2 Tbsp	black cocoa powder
CHOCOLATE PÂTE À CHOUX	
¼ cup [60 g]	water
¼ cup [60 g]	whole milk
4 Tbsp [57 g]	unsalted butter, cubed
2 tsp	granulated sugar
½ tsp	vanilla extract
¼ tsp	kosher salt
½ cup [65 g]	bread flour or all-purpose flour
2 Tbsp	Dutch-process cocoa powder, sifted
½ cup [120 g]	eggs, beaten (about 2½ eggs)

NOTE ○ Bread flour will result in a sturdier choux, but you can use all-purpose flour if you don't have bread flour!

Cookies and cream will always have a special place in my heart. So, of course, I had to recreate the classic flavor combination in a cream puff. The airy chocolate choux, crispy black cocoa craquelin cookie, and luscious white chocolate namelaka cream with bits of crushed cookies make this cream puff a winning combination of flavors and textures. The star of this puff is the namelaka, which directly translates to "creamy" in Japanese and was invented by l'École Valrhona. In this mix between ganache and mousse, the high amount of cream yields a velvety, ethereal texture that melts in your mouth. Even better, namelaka is quite easy to make, since it doesn't contain any eggs or flour and uses powdered gelatin to help it set and do all the work.

DIRECTIONS

1 **For the White Chocolate Namelaka:** In a small bowl, stir the powdered gelatin with 1 Tbsp of cold water until combined; let it bloom for 5 minutes.

2 Place the chopped white chocolate in a large heatproof mixing bowl.

3 In a small saucepan over medium heat, combine the milk, vanilla, and salt and bring to a boil. Remove from the heat and stir in the bloomed gelatin. Whisk until completely dissolved, then pour over the chopped chocolate in several additions, thoroughly mixing between each addition. Set aside. →

4 In a small saucepan over medium heat, gently heat the heavy cream until it's about 110°F [45°C]. Add the warm cream to the chocolate mixture and whisk until fully incorporated and the chocolate is fully melted. For a silky-smooth texture, use an immersion blender to emulsify the mixture for 30 seconds. Add the mascarpone (cold, straight from the fridge is okay) and blend until smooth and homogenous, about 1 minute. Check to make sure there are no lumps of mascarpone left and the mixture is smooth. Scrape down the bowl and place plastic wrap directly onto the surface of the namelaka to prevent a skin from forming. Chill in the refrigerator for at least 4 hours or overnight.

5 **For the Chocolate Craquelin Cookie:** In a stand mixer fitted with the paddle attachment, beat the butter, sugar, and salt on low speed until light and fluffy. Scrape down bowl and add the flour and black cocoa powder and mix until combined.

6 Mound the cookie dough between two sheets of parchment paper. Roll out the dough between two pieces of parchment paper to approximately ⅛ in [3 mm] thick. Don't worry too much about the shape since we'll be cutting out rounds. Transfer the cookie dough to a baking sheet and freeze until firm, 15 to 20 minutes.

7 **For the Chocolate Pâte à Choux:** In a medium saucepan over medium heat, combine the water, milk, butter, sugar, vanilla, and salt and bring to a rolling boil. Immediately remove from the heat and sift in the flour and cocoa powder.

8 Whisk until there are no lumps in the dough. Gently shake the dough off the whisk and then switch to a rubber spatula.

9 Return the saucepan to medium heat and cook for 2 minutes, stirring constantly with the spatula. You know the dough is ready when you see a thin skin form on the bottom of the pot and the dough has formed into a ball. This ensures you have evaporated some of the moisture.

10 Transfer the dough to the bowl of a stand mixer fitted with the paddle attachment. Mix on low speed until the steam dissipates and the dough cools down to 140°F [60°C] but is still warm, to avoid cooking the eggs. With the mixer running on low speed, add the eggs in three additions, ensuring each one is fully incorporated before adding the next. The dough will look curdled, but rest assured it will come together within a few seconds. Scrape down the bowl in between each egg addition to make sure everything is well combined. Mix on medium speed for another 2 minutes to ensure everything is incorporated and the dough is hydrated and has cooled. The final consistency should be pipeable and not too stiff.

11 **To Assemble:** Preheat the oven to 375°F [190°C]. Line two baking sheets with parchment paper.

12 Transfer the choux to a pastry bag fitted with a ½ in [13 mm] round tip. Pipe out balls about 1½ in [4 cm] in diameter onto the prepared baking sheets, spacing them a few inches apart.

13 Remove the craquelin from the freezer and cut circles using a 2 in [5 cm] round cutter. Use a small offset spatula to carefully loosen the rounds from the parchment paper. Gently top each choux with a craquelin cookie.

14 Lower the oven temperature to 350°F [175°C] and immediately place the baking sheets in the oven. Bake for 30 to 35 minutes, then lower the oven temperature again to 325°F [160°C] and bake for an additional 10 minutes. This method of modulating the temperature helps give the choux oven spring in the beginning and also ensures they're dried out to achieve a light and airy puff. Transfer the baking sheets to a wire rack and let cool completely before filling.

15 Just before you're ready to fill the cream puffs, finely chop the Oreos into small pieces. Alternatively, transfer the cookies to a plastic bag and crush with a rolling pin until finely ground. The pieces should be smaller than the diameter of the pastry tip so you can freely pipe the cream into the choux. Remove the namelaka cream from the refrigerator and whip with an electric hand mixer until light and fluffy. Fold in the cookie crumbs and mix until combined.

16 Fit a pastry bag with a small round tip and fill it with the namelaka cream. Using the tip of a small knife, poke a hole in the bottom of each puff, and then pipe the namelaka into the puff. Serve immediately or within a few hours. Cream puffs are best eaten fresh.

BRIOCHE SUISSE

MAKES 8 BRIOCHE SUISSE	
BRIOCHE	
2 cups [250 g]	bread flour, plus more for dusting
3 Tbsp	granulated sugar
1½ tsp	instant yeast
1 tsp	kosher salt
3	eggs, beaten, plus 1 egg beaten, for the egg wash
½ cup [115 g]	unsalted butter, cubed, at room temperature
PASTRY CREAM	
3	egg yolks
¼ cup [50 g]	granulated sugar, divided
3 Tbsp	cornstarch
1 cup [240 g]	whole milk, divided
2 Tbsp	unsalted butter, at room temperature
1 tsp	vanilla extract
⅓ cup [60 g]	mini semisweet chocolate chips

Brioche Suisse is a delectable pastry that will elevate your mornings with its sweet and buttery goodness. This classic pastry is made with an enriched brioche dough filled with vanilla pastry cream and a generous scattering of chocolate chips. It's the perfect weekend treat when you're craving something special or want to impress guests. I like to make the dough and pastry cream the day before, making assembly easy in the morning. Best enjoyed with a cup of coffee for breakfast or as an afternoon treat, these are sure to make your day brighter and transport you to Paris.

DIRECTIONS

1   **For the Brioche:** In the bowl of a stand mixer, add the flour, sugar, yeast, and salt; do not whisk. Add the 3 beaten eggs to the bowl. Fit the mixer with the dough hook attachment and mix on low speed until incorporated, then increase the speed to medium. Knead for 10 to 15 minutes, until the dough starts to pull away from the sides of the bowl and develops elasticity. Scrape down the bowl to ensure any dry bits are incorporated. With the mixer running on low speed, slowly add the butter pieces to the dough, one at a time, waiting until each piece is incorporated. Be patient and do not add it all at once or you may break the gluten structure. Once the butter is fully incorporated, mix again on medium speed for another 10 minutes, or until the dough is smooth, elastic like a rubber band, and clearing the sides of the bowl. →

2   Lightly grease a bowl or quart container with nonstick spray and transfer the dough into the bowl. Cover the bowl with plastic wrap or a clean dish towel and let rise for 2 hours at room temperature or until it has doubled in size.

3   Once the dough has doubled in size, punch the dough to degas it, then cover it with plastic wrap and put in the refrigerator to chill overnight.

4   **For the Pastry Cream:** In a large bowl, whisk together the egg yolks, 2 Tbsp of the sugar, and the cornstarch. Add a few Tbsp of the milk to thin it out and whisk to combine.

5   In a medium saucepan over medium heat, bring the remaining milk and the remaining 2 Tbsp of sugar to a boil. Remove from the heat and slowly stream the milk mixture into the egg mixture while whisking constantly. This will temper the eggs.

6   Pour the tempered egg mixture back into the saucepan and cook over medium heat, whisking constantly, until the mixture starts to thicken and boil. Cook for 1 minute to cook off any raw cornstarch flavor. Strain the mixture through a fine-mesh sieve into a medium bowl, then add the butter and vanilla. Whisk or use an immersion blender to emulsify. Place plastic wrap directly onto the surface of the custard to prevent a skin from forming. Chill in the refrigerator for at least 4 hours or overnight.

7   **To Assemble:** Line a baking sheet with parchment paper. Remove the dough from the refrigerator and transfer to a lightly floured work surface. Roll the dough into a 10 by 16 in [25 by 40.5 cm] rectangle. If the dough is tough to roll, let it rest for 5 to 10 minutes to help the gluten relax.

8   Spread the pastry cream over half of the dough, lengthwise, leaving a ¼ in [6 mm] border on three sides. Evenly sprinkle the pastry cream with mini chocolate chips. Fold the uncovered half of the dough over the cream and gently seal the open sides using your fingers. Cut into eight 5 by 2 in [13 by 5 cm] pieces. Transfer to the prepared baking sheet and arrange 2 in [5 cm] apart. Loosely cover with plastic wrap and proof at room temperature for 1 hour.

9   About 20 minutes before you're ready to bake, preheat the oven to 350°F [175°C].

10   In a small bowl, lightly beat the remaining egg with 1 Tbsp of water. Brush the brioche with the egg wash and bake for 15 to 20 minutes or until golden brown and the dough registers 200°F [93°C].

11   Transfer the baking sheet to a wire rack and let cool before serving. Brioche Suisse are best eaten the day they are made. Store any leftovers in an airtight container in the fridge for up to 2 days.

CHOCOLATE PISTACHIO PRALINE MARITOZZI

MAKES 12 BUNS	
CHOCOLATE CREAM	
4 oz [115 g]	60% dark chocolate, chopped
1½ cups [360 g]	heavy cream, divided
¼ cup [30 g]	confectioners' sugar, sifted
PISTACHIO PRALINE	
1 cup [145 g]	pistachios
½ cup [100 g]	granulated sugar
MARITOZZI DOUGH	
¼ cup [60 g]	whole milk
2	eggs, plus 1 egg, for the egg wash
2 cups [250 g]	bread flour, plus more for dusting
¼ cup [50 g]	granulated sugar
2¼ tsp	instant yeast
1 tsp	kosher salt
½ cup [115 g]	unsalted butter, cubed, at room temperature
ASSEMBLY	
12	fresh raspberries

Maritozzi are Italian brioche pastries with roots originating in Rome. Historically made only during Lent, they are now enjoyed at breakfast or as a mid-afternoon treat. The Pac-Man shaped pastries have evolved over the years, serving as a versatile canvas for a variety of fillings, both sweet and savory. From luscious creams and candied peels to a medley of nuts, these pastries can be tailored to suit any palate, making them a delightful treat for all to enjoy. My version of these soft and pillowy buns are filled with a nutty pistachio praline paste and chocolate whipped cream, resulting in an elegant, not-too-sweet treat. I also like to tuck a raspberry in the center as a surprise burst of flavor.

1 **For the Chocolate Cream:** Melt the chocolate over a double boiler (see page 14).

2 In a small saucepan over medium heat, bring ½ cup [120 g] of the heavy cream to a boil. Pour over the melted chocolate and whisk until homogeneous. Add the remaining 1 cup [240 g] of heavy cream and mix with an immersion blender until smooth and emulsified. Transfer to a container and chill in the refrigerator for at least 4 hours or overnight. →

3 **For the Pistachio Praline:** Preheat the oven to 250°C [120°C]. Line a baking sheet with parchment paper.

4 Place the pistachios on another baking sheet and lightly toast for 20 minutes, until fragrant.

5 In a small saucepan, combine the sugar and ¼ cup [60 g] of water. Using your index finger, gently incorporate the water into the sugar until the mixture resembles wet sand. Wet your hand and clean the sides of the saucepan to remove any remaining dry bits of sugar. Heat the sugar over medium heat (do not stir yet!) and then add the pistachios once the sugar has melted. Cook until the caramel turns a deep amber color and stir the pistachios until evenly coated in the caramelized sugar, 5 to 7 minutes.

6 Pour the mixture onto the prepared baking sheet, spread it out in an even layer, and let cool completely. Once cooled, break the praline into pieces and transfer to a food processor. Pulse into a smooth paste, 5 to 7 minutes. If needed, take a break halfway to give the food processor motor a rest. The longer you process, the smoother the paste will become, so be patient! For a thinner consistency, add 1 to 2 Tbsp neutral oil.

7 **For the Maritozzi Dough:** In the bowl of a stand mixer fitted with the dough hook attachment, add the milk and 2 eggs, followed by the flour, sugar, yeast, and salt. Mix on low speed until incorporated, then increase the speed to medium. Knead for 10 to 15 minutes, until the dough starts to pull away from the sides of the bowl and develops elasticity. Scrape down the bowl to ensure any dry bits are incorporated.

8 With the mixer running on low speed, slowly add the butter pieces one at a time, waiting until each piece is incorporated. Be patient and do not add it all at once or you may break the gluten structure. If needed, scrape down the bowl to make sure all the butter is incorporated. Once the butter is fully incorporated, mix again on medium speed for another 10 minutes, or until the dough is smooth, elastic like a rubber band, and clears the sides of the bowl.

9 Lightly grease a bowl or quart container with nonstick spray and transfer the dough to the bowl. Cover the bowl with plastic wrap or a clean dish towel and let it rise for 1 hour at room temperature or until it has doubled in size.

10 Once doubled in size, punch the dough to degas it, then cover it tightly with plastic wrap and refrigerate overnight to ferment. $\rightarrow$

11 **To Assemble:** Line a baking sheet with parchment paper. Transfer the dough to a lightly floured work surface and divide into 12 pieces, about 1½ oz [45 g] each. Using the heel of your palm, gently flatten a piece of dough, bring the corners together into the middle, and roll it into a tight, smooth ball. Place seam-side down on the prepared baking sheet and cover with plastic wrap or a kitchen towel. Repeat with the remaining dough and let proof for 20 to 30 minutes.

12 Roll each ball again by flattening, folding the corners into the middle, and rolling into a ball, applying firm pressure with the cup of your hand. Arrange the dough balls seam-side down on the baking sheet, allowing a few inches of space between them. Lightly cover with plastic wrap and let rise for 45 minutes to 1 hour at room temperature, or until risen by half.

13 About 20 minutes before you're ready to bake, preheat the oven to 350°F [175°C].

14 Lightly beat the remaining egg with 1 Tbsp of water in a small bowl and brush each dough ball with the egg wash. Bake for 15 to 20 minutes, until golden brown and the dough registers 200°F [93°C]. Transfer the baking sheet to a wire rack to cool completely.

15 Whip the chocolate cream with a hand mixer until light and soft peaks form. Cut each maritozzi bun in half, leaving a hinge intact like a Pac-Man. Spread about 1 to 2 tsp of pistachio praline in the hinged part of the bun, place a fresh raspberry in the center, and fill the bun with the chocolate cream, using a knife to smooth the cream along the edges. Maritozzi are best served fresh and eaten the day they are made. If you have any leftovers, store in an airtight container in the fridge for up to 2 days.

VARIATION

Nutella Maritozzi: Substitute the pistachio praline with Nutella for a hazelnut chocolate combination!

CHOCOLATE CRÉMEUX ÉCLAIRS

MAKES 12 TO 14 ÉCLAIRS	
CHOCOLATE CRÉMEUX	
8 oz [225 g]	60% to 70% dark chocolate, finely chopped
6	egg yolks
⅓ cup plus 1 Tbsp [80 g]	granulated sugar, divided
1 cup [240 g]	heavy cream
1 cup [240 g]	whole milk
½ tsp	kosher salt
1 tsp	vanilla extract
SALTED CARAMEL	
½ cup [100 g]	granulated sugar
¼ cup [57 g]	unsalted butter, cubed
¼ cup [60 g]	heavy cream
1 tsp	vanilla extract
½ tsp	kosher salt
PÂTE À CHOUX	
7 Tbsp [105 g]	water
7 Tbsp [105 g]	whole milk
7 Tbsp [100 g]	unsalted butter, cubed
2 tsp	granulated sugar
1 tsp	vanilla extract
½ tsp	kosher salt
1 cup [125 g]	bread flour or all-purpose flour
4	eggs
Confectioners' sugar, for dusting	
CHOCOLATE GLAZE	
4 oz [115 g]	60% dark chocolate, finely chopped
½ cup [120 g]	heavy cream
1 tsp	honey

NOTE ○ Bread flour will result in a sturdier choux, but all-purpose flour works too!

Éclairs are particularly sentimental to me. Every time my dad and I would go grocery shopping together, we always found ourselves at the bakery located next door to the grocery store. We'd each pick a chocolate éclair for dessert and a freshly baked cookie for the road as a reward for running errands. It became our weekend ritual until the bakery closed down. I've transformed this special treat into a double chocolate delight. Instead of traditional pastry cream, I've opted for a rich and velvety chocolate crémeux to add a touch of decadence. *Crémeux* means "creamy" in French and it is made by emulsifying chocolate with a crème anglaise. The result is a smooth, ethereal filling reminiscent of chocolate ice cream. Paired with salted caramel to create the perfect balance of sweet and salty, these éclairs are sure to impress.

DIRECTIONS

1 **For the Chocolate Crémeux:** Place the chocolate in a large heatproof mixing bowl. Set aside. In a second large heatproof mixing bowl, combine the egg yolks and half of the sugar.

2 In a medium saucepan over medium heat, bring the cream, milk, salt, and the remaining sugar to a boil. Slowly pour the hot cream mixture in a steady stream over the egg yolk mixture while whisking constantly to temper the egg yolks. →

3   Transfer the mixture back to the saucepan and cook over low heat until the mixture reaches 183°F [85°C], whisking constantly. The crème anglaise should be thick and coat the back of a spoon. Pour the crème anglaise over the chopped chocolate. Let sit for 1 minute, then add the vanilla and whisk until combined and smooth. Use an immersion blender for a silky texture. Scrape down the bowl and place a piece of plastic wrap directly onto the crémeux to prevent a skin from forming. Transfer to the refrigerator and chill for at least 4 hours or overnight.

4   **For the Salted Caramel:** In a medium saucepan, add the sugar and 2 Tbsp of water. Using your index finger, gently incorporate the water into the sugar until the mixture resembles wet sand. Wet your hand and clean the sides of the saucepan to remove any remaining dry bits of sugar. Heat the sugar over medium heat until the sugar turns a deep amber color, 10 to 15 minutes. Resist the urge to stir, as stirring will agitate the sugar crystals and cause the sugar to seize up.

5   Once the caramel reaches an amber color, immediately remove from the heat and carefully add the butter and then the cream. Be careful of the steam as the caramel rapidly bubbles up and sputters. Return the caramel to medium heat and cook, whisking constantly, until the caramel reaches 225°F [107°C] on a candy thermometer. Remove from the heat and whisk in the vanilla and salt. Transfer to a container and allow to cool completely to room temperature.

6   **For the Pâte à Choux:** In a medium saucepan over medium heat, combine the water, milk, butter, sugar, vanilla, and salt and bring to a rolling boil. Immediately remove from the heat and sift in the flour all at once. Whisk until there are no lumps in the dough. Gently shake the dough off the whisk and then switch to a rubber spatula.

7   Return the dough to medium heat and cook for 2 minutes, stirring constantly with the spatula. You know the dough is ready when you see a thin skin form on the bottom of the pot and the dough has formed into a ball. This ensures you have evaporated some of the moisture.

8   Transfer the dough to the bowl of a stand mixer fitted with the paddle attachment. Mix on low speed until the steam dissipates and the dough cools down to 140°F [60°C] but is still warm to avoid cooking the eggs. With the mixer running on low speed, add the eggs one at a time, ensuring each one is fully incorporated before adding the next. The dough will look curdled, but rest assured it will come together within a few seconds. Be sure to scrape down the bowl in between each egg addition to make sure everything is well combined. Mix on medium speed for another 2 minutes to ensure everything is incorporated and the dough is hydrated and has cooled. The final consistency should be pipeable and not too stiff.   →

9   **To Assemble:** Preheat the oven to 375°F [190°C]. Line two baking sheets with parchment paper.

10   Transfer the choux to a pastry bag fitted with a French star tip. (I recommend Ateco #867.) The ridges on this shape will help reduce any cracking as the choux expands while it bakes. If you have only a round tip, you can lightly run the tines of a fork through the piped choux to create ridges.

11   Pipe the choux into 5 in [13 cm] lines, holding the piping bag at a 45-degree angle, spacing them 2 in [5 cm] apart on the prepared baking sheets. (If needed, mark the underside of the parchment paper with 5 in [13 cm] lines to help guide you.) Dust confectioners' sugar over the tops of each choux (this will help with browning but won't ruin the ridges like an egg wash would).

12   Lower the oven temperature to 350°F [175°C] and immediately place the choux into the oven. Bake for 45 to 50 minutes, then lower the oven temperature again to 325°F [160°C] and bake for an additional 10 minutes. (This method of modulating the temperature helps give the éclairs oven spring in the beginning and also ensures they're dried out to achieve a light and airy puff.)

13   Cut a slit in the bottom of each éclair with a paring knife to release steam and prevent them from getting soggy. Transfer the baking sheets to a wire rack and let cool completely before filling.

14   Fit a pastry bag with a small round tip and fill with the chocolate crémeux. Fit another pastry bag with a small round tip and fill with the salted caramel. Using the tip of a small knife, poke three holes in the bottom of each éclair, and then pipe the crémeux until almost full. Pipe the salted caramel into the éclairs until full.

15   **For the Chocolate Glaze:** Melt the chocolate over a double boiler (see page 14).

16   In a small saucepan over medium heat, bring the cream to a boil. Gradually pour the hot cream over the melted chocolate and add the honey. Whisk until emulsified, then let cool to room temperature.

17   Working with one éclair at a time, dip the top into the glaze, then return to the baking sheet. Repeat with remaining éclairs. Allow the glaze to set at room temperature, about 30 minutes. Éclairs are best eaten fresh. Store any leftovers in an airtight container in the fridge for up to 2 days.

BLACK SESAME COCOA MILK BREAD

MAKES 8 KNOTS	
TANGZHONG	
3 Tbsp [25 g]	bread flour
½ cup [120 g]	whole milk
MILK BREAD DOUGH	
½ cup [120 g]	whole milk, warmed to 110°F [45°C]
1	egg, at room temperature
1	egg yolk, at room temperature
2¾ cups [345 g]	bread flour
⅓ cup [67 g]	granulated sugar
2¼ tsp	instant yeast
1¼ tsp	kosher salt
¼ cup [57 g]	unsalted butter, cubed, at room temperature
BLACK SESAME COCOA FILLING	
5 Tbsp [38 g]	black sesame seeds, toasted
½ cup [100 g]	granulated sugar
¼ cup [20 g]	Dutch-process cocoa powder, sifted
6 Tbsp [85 g]	unsalted butter, at room temperature
Sweetened condensed milk, for drizzling (optional)	

To say I am obsessed with Japanese milk bread is an understatement. The plush, tender texture of milk bread is unparalleled, and it's all thanks to the tangzhong, a cooked roux made from milk and flour that tenderizes the dough and helps retain moisture, preventing the bread from getting dry and stale. The dough's versatility allows for endless adaptations, and these braided knots are one of my absolute favorites with their beautiful striations and braids of black sesame. The cocoa adds a very subtle hint of chocolate that works so well with the sweet, nutty black sesame. This ultra-soft, enriched dough can be used for cinnamon rolls, sweet buns, loafs—you name it. Give it a go!

DIRECTIONS

1 **For the Tangzhong:** In a small saucepan, whisk together the bread flour and milk to remove any lumps. Cook over medium-low heat, whisking constantly, for 3 to 5 minutes, until the roux starts to thicken and reaches 150°F [65°C]. The roux should have the consistency of a curd. Remove from the heat and let cool slightly.

2 **For the Milk Bread Dough:** In the bowl of a stand mixer fitted with the dough hook, add the warm milk, egg, egg yolk, and tangzhong. Then add the bread flour, sugar, instant yeast, and salt. Mix on medium-low speed for 10 to 15 minutes, until gluten develops and the dough feels elastic. →

3   Add the butter 1 Tbsp at a time and mix until the butter is completely incorporated. This may take a while, so be patient and use a wet rubber spatula to scrape down the bowl when necessary. Once all the butter is incorporated, mix for another 7 to 10 minutes or until the dough is smooth and elastic. The dough will be a bit tacky, but should feel elastic like a rubber band, which indicates good gluten structure.

4   Using wet hands, shape the dough into a ball and transfer it to a greased bowl or container. Cover and let rise until doubled in size, 45 to 60 minutes, depending on how warm your house is. Be sure to keep an eye on it because it can go fast if it's hot outside!

5   **For the Black Sesame Cocoa Filling:** In a spice grinder or coffee grinder, blitz the sesame seeds into a powder. Add the sugar and blitz again. Transfer the mixture to a small mixing bowl, add the cocoa powder and softened butter, and mix until homogeneous and it becomes a soft, spreadable paste.

6   **To Assemble:** Transfer the dough to a lightly floured work surface, pat it into a rectangle, and roll it into an 18 by 13 in [46 by 33 cm] rectangle. Spread an even layer of the filling over the dough, leaving a ¼ in [6 mm] border along one long side. Fold the dough into thirds: Starting with the long side that doesn't have the exposed border, fold it over the middle. Then pick up the opposite side with the ¼ in [6 mm] border and gently fold and stretch it on top of the first third of the dough. Pinch the top seam together, trim the short edges, and gently roll the dough with a rolling pin to remove any air bubbles. The folded dough should be approximately 16 by 4 in [40.5 by 10 cm].

7   Line a baking sheet with parchment paper.

8   With a pizza cutter or a very sharp knife, cut the dough into 8 equal 2 by 4 in [5 by 10 cm] strips. Carefully transfer the strips to the prepared baking sheet and chill in the freezer for 10 to 15 minutes to help firm up both the dough and filling, making it easier and less messy to work with. Meanwhile, grease the two outer columns of a muffin tin for a total of 8 greased wells, leaving the middle column empty. This will give the knots room to expand while baking.   →

9   Working with one piece of dough at a time, carefully peel the strip of dough away from the parchment paper (the dough will be quite sticky) and gently stretch the dough lengthwise into a 2 by 5 in [5 by 13 cm] rectangle. On a lightly floured work surface, cut two slits down most of the length of each strip to make three strands, cutting only about 90 percent of the way through the length of the dough, leaving the top of the dough intact. Braid each strand of dough, alternating right and left over center, and then gently pinch the ends of the braid together. Starting from the top of the intact side, roll the dough lengthwise like you would a sleeping bag to make a ball. Transfer the dough ball to the greased muffin tin with the braid facing up. Repeat with the remaining dough. Cover and allow to proof at room temperature for 45 minutes to 1 hour, depending on the temperature in your house.

10   About 20 minutes before you're ready to bake, preheat the oven to 350°F [175°C]. Bake for 15 to 20 minutes or until the internal temperature of the dough reaches 195°F [90°C]. Transfer to a wire rack and let cool in the muffin tin. Serve warm and enjoy these soft, pillowy knots! I think they're good on their own, but if you're craving a little extra sweetness, then drizzle with a little sweetened condensed milk. Store any leftovers in an airtight container at room temperature for up to 3 days.

PEANUT BUTTER CHOCOLATE BUNS

MAKES 12 BUNS	
CHOCOLATE PEANUT BUTTER FILLING	
4 oz [115 g]	bittersweet or semisweet chocolate, chopped
¼ cup [57 g]	unsalted butter, at room temperature
¼ cup [65 g]	creamy peanut butter
½ cup [100 g]	light brown sugar, packed
2 tsp	ground cinnamon
½ tsp	vanilla extract
BRIOCHE DOUGH	
1 cup [240 g]	whole milk, warmed to 110°F [45°C]
3	large eggs
1 tsp	vanilla extract
4½ cups [565 g]	all-purpose flour, plus more for dusting
½ cup [100 g]	granulated sugar
2¼ tsp	instant yeast
2 tsp	kosher salt
½ cup [115 g]	unsalted butter, cubed, at room temperature
PEANUT BUTTER CREAM CHEESE FROSTING	
4 oz [115 g]	cream cheese, at room temperature
¼ cup [57 g]	unsalted butter, at room temperature
2 Tbsp	creamy peanut butter
1½ cups [180 g]	confectioners' sugar, sifted
2 Tbsp	whole milk
½ tsp	vanilla extract

Waking up to the warm, comforting aroma of freshly baked buns is one of the best ways to start the day. Made with a super-enriched brioche dough, these rolls are filled with a decadent chocolate peanut butter filling and topped with a luscious peanut butter cream cheese frosting. The key to achieving that signature gooey center is slightly underbaking them so they don't dry out. These buns are always my go-to during the holidays or when I have company because the dough and filling can be made the day before. Then, all I have to do is simply assemble and bake until golden brown in the morning, making me look like an absolute hero.

DIRECTIONS

1 **For the Chocolate Peanut Butter Filling:** Melt the chocolate over a double boiler (see page 14), remove from heat, and set aside.

2 In a stand mixer fitted with the paddle attachment or in a large bowl using a hand mixer, mix together the butter, peanut butter, sugar, cinnamon, and vanilla. Add the melted chocolate and mix until combined. Cover and set aside until ready to use. If making ahead, cover tightly and refrigerate for up to 2 days, then let come to room temperature for 1 hour before using. →

3 **For the Brioche Dough:** In the bowl of a stand mixer fitted with the dough hook attachment, add the warm milk, eggs, and vanilla, followed by the flour, sugar, yeast, and salt. Mix on low speed until incorporated, then increase the speed to medium. Knead for 10 to 15 minutes, until the dough starts to pull away from the sides of the bowl and develops elasticity.

4 Scrape down the bowl to ensure any dry bits are incorporated. With the mixer running on low speed, slowly add the butter pieces, one at a time, waiting until each piece is incorporated. Be patient and do not add it all at once or you may break the gluten structure. If needed, stop to scrape down the bowl to make sure all the butter is incorporated. Once the butter is fully incorporated, mix again on medium speed for another 10 minutes, or until the dough is smooth, elastic like a rubber band, and clears the sides of the bowl.

5 Lightly grease a bowl or quart container with nonstick spray and transfer the dough to the bowl. Cover the bowl with plastic wrap or a clean dish towel and let the dough rise for 1 hour at room temperature or until it has doubled in size. Once doubled in size, punch the dough to degas it, then cover it tightly with plastic wrap and refrigerate overnight to ferment.

6 **To Assemble:** One hour before assembling, bring the filling back to room temperature if you made it ahead.

7 Transfer the dough to a lightly floured work surface and roll it into a 16 by 12 in [40.5 by 30 cm] rectangle. Spread an even layer of the filling over the dough, leaving a ¼ in [6 mm]

border along a long side. Starting with the filling-covered long side, roll the dough into a tight log and pinch the seam closed with your fingers. Lightly score and cut the dough into eight equal 1½ to 2 in [4 to 5 cm] pieces using a sharp knife.

8 Place the buns onto a parchment paper–lined baking sheet, spaced evenly apart. Cover the buns with lightly greased plastic wrap and let rise at room temperature for 1 to 2 hours (depending on the warmth of your kitchen), until doubled in size. While the buns are proofing, make the frosting.

9 **For the Peanut Butter Cream Cheese Frosting:** In the bowl of a stand mixer fitted with the paddle attachment or in a large bowl with a hand mixer, cream together the cream cheese, butter, and peanut butter. Add the sugar, milk, and vanilla and mix, starting on low speed and gradually increasing to medium speed once incorporated. Beat until smooth and fluffy, about 2 to 3 minutes.

10 **To Bake:** About 20 minutes before you're ready to bake, preheat the oven to 350°F [175°C]. Remove the plastic wrap and bake the buns for 25 to 30 minutes, or until golden brown and the internal temperature reaches 190°F [88°C] on an instant-read thermometer.

11 Transfer to a wire rack and let cool for 10 minutes on the baking sheet before spreading the frosting over the tops of the buns. Eat while still slightly warm for maximum gooeyness. Store leftovers, covered, at room temperature for up to 2 days or in the refrigerator for up to 4 days.

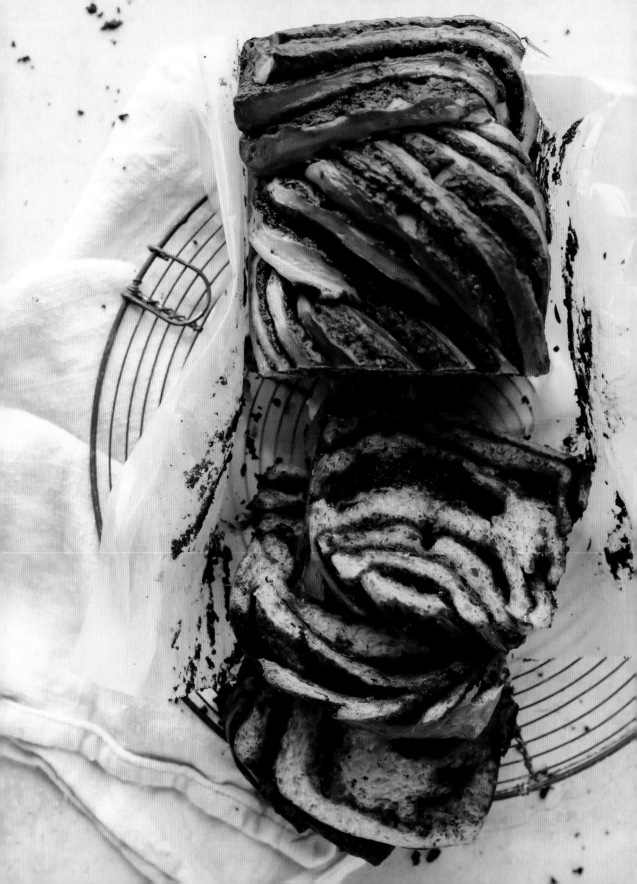

PUMPKIN CHOCOLATE BABKA

MAKES TWO 9 BY 5 IN [23 BY 13 CM] BABKAS	
PUMPKIN BABKA DOUGH	
4½ cups [565 g]	all-purpose flour, plus more for dusting
½ cup [100 g]	granulated sugar
2¼ tsp	instant yeast
1 tsp	kosher salt
¾ cup [180 g]	pumpkin purée, patted dry
2	large eggs
1 tsp	vanilla extract
¾ cup [180 g]	whole milk, warmed to about 95°F [35°C]
½ cup [115 g]	unsalted butter, at room temperature
CHOCOLATE FILLING	
4 oz [115 g]	bittersweet or semisweet chocolate, chopped
½ cup [115 g]	unsalted butter, at room temperature
½ cup [100 g]	light brown sugar, packed
¼ cup [20 g]	unsweetened or Dutch-process cocoa powder
½ tsp	kosher salt
¼ tsp	ground cinnamon
1 tsp	vanilla extract
SIMPLE SYRUP	
½ cup [100 g]	granulated sugar
ASSEMBLY	
1 cup [115 g]	toasted pecans, chopped (optional)

While I didn't grow up with babkas, I did grow up watching *Seinfeld*. One of my favorite episodes is when Jerry and Elaine declare the chocolate babka as the superior babka and all others as lesser. But what about a pumpkin chocolate babka? I'd say it rivals the classic and makes for the perfect fall treat. Made from an enriched yeasted sweet dough (or sometimes laminated dough), this beloved Eastern European bread is filled, braided, and baked in a loaf pan. The top is brushed with a simple syrup that keeps the bread moist and creates a shiny, golden-brown sheen. Its signature layers of exposed chocolate swirls will lure you in upon first glance. If the process seems too daunting or intimidating, you can break it up into two stages. Make the simple syrup and chocolate filling one day and then make the dough, assemble it, and bake it the following day.

DIRECTIONS

1 **For the Pumpkin Babka Dough:** In a large bowl, combine the flour, sugar, yeast, and salt. →

2   In the bowl of a stand mixer fitted with the dough hook, add the pumpkin purée, eggs, and vanilla. Pour in the warm milk, then add the flour mixture on top. Turn the mixer on low speed and mix until the ingredients are incorporated, 2 to 3 minutes. Increase the speed to medium and mix for an additional 10 minutes or until the dough has some tension. Slowly add the butter one Tbsp at a time, waiting about 30 seconds between each addition, continuing to mix until the butter is fully incorporated. Mix for another 5 minutes or until the dough is smooth, shiny, and elastic and doesn't stick to the sides of the bowl. You'll know it's ready when the dough feels like it has some tension, like a rubber band.

3   Transfer the dough to a lightly greased bowl and cover with a clean towel or plastic wrap. Let the dough rise in a warm place until it doubles in size, 1 to 2 hours, depending on the warmth of your kitchen. In the meantime, make the chocolate filling and sugar syrup.

4   **For the Chocolate Filling:** Melt the chocolate over a double boiler (see page 14). Remove from the heat and set aside for 2 minutes.

5   In a stand mixer fitted with the paddle attachment or using a hand mixer, mix the butter, sugar, cocoa powder, salt, cinnamon, and vanilla. Add the melted chocolate and mix until combined. Cover and set aside until ready to use. If making ahead, cover tightly and refrigerate for up to 2 days, then let come to room temperature for 1 hour before using.

6   **For the Simple Syrup:** In a small saucepan over medium heat combine ½ cup [120 g] of water and the sugar. Simmer until the sugar has dissolved, about 2 minutes. Remove from the heat and set aside to cool.

7 **To Assemble:** Grease two 9 by 5 in [23 by 13 cm] loaf pans and line with parchment paper, leaving a 1 in [2.5 cm] overhang on two sides.

8 Gently punch down the dough to deflate, divide it in half, and cover with a kitchen towel. Working with one half at a time, roll the dough into a 10 by 18 in [25 by 46 cm] rectangle, about ¼ in [6 mm] thick on a lightly floured work surface. Spread half of the chocolate filling over the dough using an offset spatula and sprinkle with half of the chopped pecans, if using.

9 Starting with a short edge, roll the dough into a log, pinching the seam closed with your fingers. Transfer the log to a baking sheet seam-side down. Repeat the process with the remaining dough. Chill the dough logs in the freezer for 15 minutes (this helps get a clean cut).

10 With a sharp knife, trim the ends of one log and then cut the log lengthwise down the middle, exposing the filling. With the exposed side facing up, braid the two halves, overlapping each piece to make a double helix. Transfer the braided dough to a prepared loaf pan, tucking the ends underneath. Repeat with the other log. Cover loosely with a kitchen towel and let proof until puffy, 1 to 1½ hours (it won't be completely doubled in size).

11 Toward the end of the proofing time, preheat the oven to 350°F [175°C].

12 Bake the loaves for 30 minutes. Brush the tops with the simple syrup, then return to the oven for another 10 to 15 minutes (for a total of 40 to 45 minutes) or until an instant-read thermometer registers 200°F [93°C]. If the tops are getting too brown while baking, tent with foil.

13 Transfer the loaves to a wire rack to cool completely in the pans. Remove the loaves from the pan before serving and then cut into slices. Cover tightly with plastic wrap and store at room temperature for up to 3 days.

ACKNOWLEDGMENTS

Thank you! I find myself overflowing with gratitude as I reflect on the incredible journey of bringing this cookbook to life. Each page is steeped in passion and dedication, and none of this would have been possible without the help and expertise of some extraordinary individuals. It's been an absolute dream working with the team at Chronicle Books, and I am thankful for this opportunity to share my recipes with fellow chocolate lovers!

Firstly, to the readers and followers of *Studio Baked*, words cannot express the depth of my gratitude. Thank you for baking from my recipes because none of this would have been possible without your support! I feel so honored and privileged to be able to share my recipes and stories with you. Thank you, thank you, thank you to every one of you!

To my editor, Claire Gilhuly, thank you for making my cookbook dreams come true! This cookbook wouldn't exist without you, and your impact extends far beyond its pages. Your unwavering support, patience, and understanding have made me feel heard and reassured throughout this wild journey. Through countless revisions, extensions, deadlines, and feedback, you have been a beacon of light and a true partner in this process.

To my literary agent, Sally Ekus, thank you for championing my work and helping me navigate this process. I am thankful for your guidance and support and feel incredibly lucky to have you and your team by my side.

To Lizzie Vaughan, I am so grateful for your artistic talent and for turning my vision into a reality. Your designs and creativity have breathed life into every page, and you've helped make this book nothing short of magical.

A heartfelt thank you to Jessica Ling, Margo Winton Parodi, Cecilia Santini, and Rebecca Springer, whose meticulous eyes for detail and copyediting have ensured that every word on the page shines. Your precision, organization, and thoughtful feedback have been crucial in making these recipes a success.

To my incredible husband, Tyler, your love and support have been constant every step of the way. As taste tester, personal grocery shopper, dedicated dishwasher, recipe tester, and therapist, you have helped make this book what it is. Thank you for cheering me on, staying up late to keep me company, and embarking on this chocolate adventure with me.

To my family, your endless support has fueled my passion for baking. Since my time at pastry school, you have been my foundation and biggest cheerleaders. Thank you for always encouraging my dreams. I love you all!

To my friends, your support means the world to me. Thank you for taste testing, answering random chocolate poll texts, liking my unsolicited (and incessant) chocolate photos and stories, and hyping me up, always! Special thanks to Anne Cullen and Jessica Milanes for recipe testing and providing invaluable feedback.

RECIPES AT A GLANCE

INDEX

CHOCOLATE LOVER

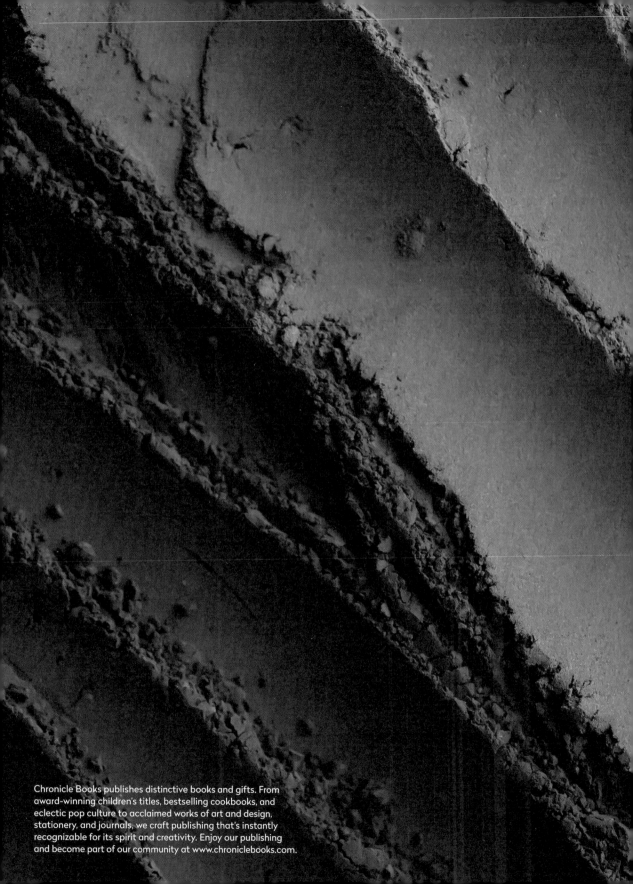

Chronicle Books publishes distinctive books and gifts. From award-winning children's titles, bestselling cookbooks, and eclectic pop culture to acclaimed works of art and design, stationery, and journals, we craft publishing that's instantly recognizable for its spirit and creativity. Enjoy our publishing and become part of our community at www.chroniclebooks.com.